Haunted Historic Colonial Williamsburg, Virginia

with Breakthrough Ghost Photography

Tim Scullion

Schiffer Publishing Ltd

4880 Lower Valley Road • Atglen, PA 19310

Other Schiffer Books on Related Subjects:

America's Historic Haunts. Linda Zimmermann.
ISBN: 978-0-7643-3700-0

Haunted Alexandria & Northern Virginia. J. J. Smith.
ISBN: 978-0-7643-3258-6

Haunted Richmond, Virginia. Pamela K. Kinney.
ISBN: 978-0-7643-2712-4

Policing the Paranormal: The Haunting of Virginia's State Capitol Complex. Paul Hope. ISBN: 978-0-7643-4320-9

Type set in Aldine721 BT/Times New Roman

ISBN: 978-0-7643-5060-3
Printed in China
Published by Schiffer Publishing, Ltd.
4880 Lower Valley Road
Atglen, PA 19310
Phone: (610) 593-1777; Fax: (610) 593-2002
E-mail: Info@schifferbooks.com
Web: www.schifferbooks.com

For our complete selection of fine books on this and related subjects, please visit our website at www.schifferbooks.com. You may also write for a free catalog.

Schiffer Publishing's titles are available at special discounts for bulk purchases for sales promotions or premiums. Special editions, including personalized covers, corporate imprints, and excerpts, can be created in large quantities for special needs. For more information, contact the publisher.

We are always looking for people to write books on new and related subjects. If you have an idea for a book, please contact us at proposals@schifferbooks.com.

Dedicated to my wife and family
for putting up with all of my late night
jaunts into Colonial Williamsburg.
Thanks to author P. A. Spade
for all the help and support.

Contents

To My Readers 6

Preface 7

What is a Ghost?

Acknowledgments....................................... 10

Chapter One: Bruton Parish Church 11

The Odyssey Begins

Chapter Two: St. George Tucker House 16

The Beautiful and the Bizarre

Chapter Three: Roscow Cole House 22

The Ghost of Christmas Present

Chapter Four: Peyton Randolph House 26

Something Wicked This Way Haunts

Chapter Five: Public Jail (Gaol) 36

13 Men in Dead Men's Coffins

Chapter Six: Elkanah Deane House 42

A Real Ghost in the Machine

Chapter Seven: Whetherburn Tavern 46

The Man Who Married and Killed for Money?

Chapter Eight: George Wythe House 50

Marriage Infidelity or Unrequited Love?

Chapter Nine: The Night Everything

Changed 55

Paranormal Reality Has Changed Completely!

Chapter Ten: John Blair House 60

The Army of the Undead Marches On

Chapter Eleven: Custis Tenement 64

The Washington Connection & the Electric Eyes

Chapter Twelve: Ludwell-Paradise

House 68

Madness and Money

Chapter Thirteen: Geddy House............. 72

Innocuous or Evil?

Chapter Fourteen: Prentis &

Tarpley Stores 76

Phantom Store Clerks . . . to Wait on You

Chapter Fifteen: President's House (College

of William & Mary).................................... 80

Thundering Down the Stairs & Slamming

Doors, or Seeping Out the Cracks?

Chapter Sixteen: Brafferton Building

(College of William & Mary) 84

Where Have all the Indian Boys Gone?

Chapter Seventeen: The Unseen

Connections 90

What Formerly Seemed Like Two is Really One!

Chapter Eighteen: Wren Building (College

of William & Mary).................................... 95

Wars, Fires & Crypts: Is Burying People Beneath

the Floor a Good Idea?

Chapter Nineteen: Bowden-Armstead

House & the Dominant Spirit................. 104

Can One Spirit Dominate Another?

Chapter Twenty: Robert Carter House 109

Horse with No Name

Chapter Twenty-One: Taliaferro-Cole

House 113

The Paranormal Gets Even More Bizarre

Chapter Twenty-Two: The Bryan House ... 117

Site of an Abduction, or Murder?

Chapter Twenty-Three: Ludwell

Tenement.. 120

Revolutionary War Soldiers Out Back?

Chapter Twenty-Four: Secretary's Office

(of the Capital)... 124

Nearsighted in Two Different Realities

Chapter Twenty-Five: Orrell House 127

The Itinerant Poltergeist

Chapter Twenty-Six: Timson House...... 130

A Different Type of Red Super Cell?

Chapter Twenty-Seven: The [Slaves']
Quarters.. 132

Ghosts . . . or Aliens?

Chapter Twenty-Eight: Ewing House 138

Which One Is Ebenezer, and What's with the Eyes?

Chapter Twenty-Nine: Benjamin Waller
House 142

Intimidation in a Window Near You!

Chapter Thirty: Robert Nicolson House ...147

One Dominant and Two Submissive . . . but
Jack, is That Your Relative?

Chapter Thirty-One: Dr. Barraud
House 152

The Doctor Is In?

Chapter Thirty-Two: Chiswell-Bucktrout
House 155

The Lady Is . . . in the Tree?

Chapter Thirty-Three: William Finney
House 160

Displaced, Distraught, and Disturbed

Chapter Thirty-Four: Thomas Nelson
House 165

Does Williamsburg's Oldest House Have its
Oldest Wraiths?

Chapter Thirty-Five: Lightfoot House..... 168

The Guardian Ghost of Presidents, Kings, and
Dignitaries

Chapter Thirty-Six: William Byrd III
House 170

For the Man Who Has Everything: Is Suicide
the Only Answer?

Chapter Thirty-Seven: Williamsburg Inn...173

Five Stars for the Afterlife

Chapter Thirty-Eight: Alexander Craig
House 177

Salacious Susanna the Spinster

Chapter Thirty-Nine: William Randolph
House 181

The Shape-Shifting Apparition

Chapter Forty: Benjamin Powell House.... 185

The Undertaker

Chapter Forty-One: Masonic Hall 188

Where is Peyton?

Chapter Forty-Two: Hunter Millinery 192

Phantoms for Fashion

Chapter Forty-Three: Churches—A Hotbed
for Paranormal Activity............................ 196

A Gathering of the Faithful . . . or the Unfaithful?

Epilogue: What I've Learned
about Ghosts 204

Trying to Understand the Unseen, the Unheard
& the Unknown

Bibliography..208

To My Readers

This book is dedicated to all of those who have to see something before they believe it. There are several books out about the ghosts of Williamsburg, Virginia—but other than a few small orbs, none of them have actual photos of the apparitions. Williamsburg has more eighteenth-century buildings (88) than any other place in America, and an additional 350 buildings reconstructed on the original foundations, making it America's largest living museum. Now to this add the 1622 Indian massacre that killed about 400 colonists, (the hardest hit being Wolstenholme Town—very close to Williamsburg on the Carter's Grove Plantation property), the mass grave of Revolutionary War soldiers unearthed at the Governor's Palace, the missing mass grave of French soldiers from the Battle of Yorktown, an unmarked pauper's graveyard on the grounds somewhere between the Bucktrout Cottage and the Williamsburg Inn, the 1862 Civil War battle that resulted in the deaths of almost 4,000 men and the mass graves associated with that battle, victims of the 1918 flu epidemic, rumors of a Native American burial ground unearthed when the Colonial Parkway Tunnel was built underneath Colonial Williamsburg, and you have more than enough evidence for my contention that it is one of America's most haunted places. This book is a look into a world we cannot see with the naked eye. The advanced electronics of the digital camera have become the eyes through which we can see evidence of the paranormal! Most ghosts, apparitions, phantoms, wraiths, or whatever you choose to call them, have an appearance like nothing you have ever imagined—are you ready for proof of an alternate reality?

Preface

The photos you are about to view are an amazing look into an alternate reality, so I would like to give you the background on how they came to be. I have been a fine arts photographer for over ten years. While photographing places in Williamsburg, Virginia, and eventually the Southwest, I came upon some anomalies in my photos that were paranormal in nature. For months I experimented with ways to expand on and perfect this technique; finally I found the right settings and gear that accomplished this task. I was able to consistently photograph paranormal apparitions of all shapes, sizes, and colors. I eagerly showed the photos to my wife, whose cool reception was indicative of a lingering doubt—I could sense that, and I'm not even psychic. However, for years I have known that my wife is what I would call a reluctant psychic. She doesn't embrace these gifts—they make her uncomfortable—but at the same time there is no denying she has them. After making what I thought was a breakthrough discovery, can you imagine my feelings when she asked, "Did you Photoshop these photographs?" My own wife did not believe me! I, of course, responded, "Absolutely not!" I asked her to come and observe a photo shoot, and several nights later she accompanied me.

One of the required stops in Colonial Williamsburg is the infamous Peyton Randolph House, with a reputation as Williamsburg's most haunted—and not in a good way! After a few minutes in front of this notorious eighteenth-century dwelling, she said, "Tim I have to go—this house is not a good place." I asked her if she saw something and she nodded yes, pointing to her arms, which were covered in goose bumps accompanied by all the tiny hairs standing straight up. I asked what she saw, and she turned to me and with a smirk said. "You are the one with the technique to photograph ghosts—you show me!" I asked her if she would at the very least tell me where she saw an apparition. I took photographs of the area she pointed out and we moved on.

A little farther down the street at the jail she again informed me that she saw a paranormal presence, but that it was not malevolent like the one at the Randolph House. Once more she told me the general location but not what she'd seen. I asked her to write down both things she had seen on a piece of paper and keep it until I processed the photos. A few hours later I called her to the studio and she brought the paper to compare what she had written to what I had captured. I photographed exactly what she had written down. She apologized but made this very astute observation: "If I was suspicious and I'm your wife, you know others will be! So you will have to put in the book how you find and edit photos (which is included in this book).

My wife is now my biggest supporter because of this experience. I expect there will be skeptics, but I can prove what I take is authentic, and the most important fact is that it is something anyone can do. Down the road I will disclose specifics on equipment, techniques, and methods so that anyone can achieve the same results, but for now I will, like a magician, keep it under wraps. I would like to be the one who gets the credit for this paranormal breakthrough. It has opened up a whole new world to someone who was a profound skeptic himself, and those who have seen this book have all said that it has changed their perception of reality. For those of you who believe that human life ends with the death of the body, you may want to rethink your philosophy: The paranormal is alive and well; existentialism may be the concept that's dead! So . . .

Come on a journey with me! I've done all the hard work, walking the damp, sometimes frigid, sometimes muggy streets in and around Williamsburg documenting the paranormal with my camera. I've spent many a late night walking these streets alone, sometimes feeling the cold chill run down my spine of something that I cannot see near me, sometimes feeling like I was being watched when I could see nothing with the naked eye, sometimes looking at what seemed like a handful of glitter being thrown all around me, realizing full well that something was so near me that I could reach out and touch it—without any idea what or who "it" was! I've documented apparitions that vary from the size of a marble to the size of a large building. I've found ghosts looking around the sides of buildings, peeking out through panes of glass, and even in the most unlikely places: a disembodied face in a bush or on the side of a chimney. I've seen hundreds of orbs floating through the sky like a small army of the undead marching to some unknown destination or dimension. I've seen orbs shape-shift in a matter of seconds from one form to completely different shapes and sizes. I feel as if these creatures are former humans locked into a new kind of existence or reality that they do not understand, and without voice boxes to speak to us, try to let us know that they are there through any means possible. I've opened up a new type of photography for those brave enough to try it—but wait—I'm getting ahead of myself. Let's go back to the beginning of this paranormal odyssey.

I have always viewed ghost stories or paranormal events with a healthy dose of skepticism. As a photographer, I began to look for something to photograph that had not been done before. I was a tour guide at Colonial Williamsburg at one time for both day and night (ghost) tours. During the "ghost tours," people using regular cell phone cameras would capture orbs, usually of the small, grey variety. I wondered if there were more possibilities to capture than just the small grey orbs. I quickly discovered that some of these "orbs" were much more than a small grey circle—they came in many different colors, shapes, and sizes. I wondered if it was my equipment, so, just to be sure, I used another brand—and got the same results. I began my new odyssey, trying to photograph and document every kind of orb or apparition that I could find, and you hold the first part of the results in your hands.

Most of the original eighteenth-century buildings (remember that "eighteenth century" means the 1700s) that have had unofficial stories of the paranormal consistently had these paranormal orbs or lights show up in photographs taken after dark. Most of the lights hover over the building or on the roof, but there are exceptions. For each photograph of a building shown, I have also shown the same photograph cropped to show the mysterious, unexplained light in question up close. No, these are not photographs that have been manipulated in Photoshop; the only adjustments that have been made are the contrast and brightness—so that the apparition can be seen a little clearer. Other than that, these are the photos as they appeared from the camera of "haunted" buildings in and around Williamsburg. This was not an easy task—it's not like you can go out any time and capture these photos. For every photo in this book, there were many times when I came home empty handed. It seems that these apparitions are very temperamental and are not always available for photo shoots. For the skeptics, I always keep a few of the best shots on my camera chip to prove that this is not just some production in Photoshop; it's straight out of the camera.

Whether you are a skeptic like I was or a believer—you cannot argue with the evidence in the pages of this book. I'm sure someone will try and give a "rational" explanation for something we do not understand, but does it really hold up? The digital camera is now our eyes into the world of the paranormal. Still, I am very curious why I cannot see these lights with my eyes and yet they show up on digital photographs. It just goes to demonstrate that for all of the technical advancements that we have made—there is still a lot that we do not know.

What Is a "Ghost"?

What is your definition of a ghost, apparition, spirit, spectre (England), wraith (Scotland), or phantom (France)? Is it perhaps an angel, a creature that represents all that is good in the universe? Is it the polar opposite: a demon, representing all that is evil in the universe? Is it the soul of a human that has died, possessing all the thoughts and personality of that human, without the physical body? What is it made of? Obviously it's not matter—so is it energy? Is it possible that it is a being that is made up of pure, intelligent, energy—as opposed to physical matter?

If you have seen real ghost photos on television or on the computer, some of them appear to be people, but have an ephemeral, misty characteristic; and they seem to appear and disappear at will. But since they do not have flesh and blood bodies, might this be an attempt on their part to retain their human appearance? As an intelligent entity that no longer has a physical mass, couldn't their appearance be normally very different from the misty humanlike appearance? Some people have seen them as little orbs of light that show up on photographs. In this book you will see more than just orbs of light that showed up on a digital camera image; you will actually see unexplained light formations that do not resemble anyone's idea of a ghost. For some reason, the digital camera can pick up these previously undetected light apparitions that are not visible to the naked eye. In Colonial Williamsburg and the surrounding area, you will see these light formations over or around historical buildings that all have rumors of ghost stories that envelop their past. Perhaps these are the normal appearances of these anomalies; perhaps they have certain color, shape, and size characteristics that make them individuals in the spirit world, just like humans living in the material world. I do believe that they try to create holograms of their former selves to let their presence be known by the living. You will see very human-like apparitions throughout this book—as well as the forms that look like someone is wearing a sheet with two eyespots. (Now I know where the traditional Halloween-type ghost comes from.) As you scroll through the pages of this study, you may have to modify your perceptions of these spirit creatures, because now you will know what they really look like! All of the atheists, agnostics, and existentialists now have something new to ponder . . . how do you explain this?

Acknowledgments

Working for several years as a tour guide in Colonial Williamsburg, I had to learn a lot of facts and dates, as well as the culture of both the eighteenth-century colonists and the Native Americans. I would like to gratefully acknowledge the historians, archeologists, and researchers of Colonial Williamsburg as my source for the background information for the buildings shown in this book. I thought that it was important to give you some background history about the house or building; if you would like to read further, check out Colonial Williamsburg's websites (start with http://www.history.org/) or their publications. From time to time, due to the discovery of new archeological evidence or documents, Colonial Williamsburg will revise their interpretation of buildings, eighteenth-century life, and history. This book was meticulously researched for accuracy through *Colonial Williamsburg's Historical Reports,* its official guide, and its *Archeological Reports.* Should any information in this book become outdated through new discoveries that I am not aware of, please notify me via Schiffer Publishing so that appropriate changes can be made (and if you do, thanks!).

CHAPTER ONE

Bruton Parish Church

The Odyssey Begins

History

In 1699, the capital of Virginia was moved from Jamestown Island, a tiny, swampy area with brackish water and little room for growth, to a place farther up the peninsula between the James and York Rivers. The place, called Middle Plantation, had its name changed to Williamsburg in honor of the reigning English monarch. A consolidated Anglican church named Bruton Parish found it necessary to build a larger church due to the influx of the governor, the Virginia legislature, students and faculty of the College of William and Mary, workers and craftsmen who would build the new capital, and all of the people associated with the government. Keep in mind that it was the law that you had to attend the Anglican Church at least once a month. Governor Spotswood drafted the plans for the cruciform-shaped (cross-shaped) church, and the Reverend James Blair, church rector and president of the College of William and Mary, supervised the construction. The church was completed in 1715, and the original building still stands today. The steeple was added a little later in the eighteenth century, as well as the Tarpley bell—cast from the same mold as Philadelphia's Liberty Bell—hence named Virginia's Liberty Bell (and it never cracked).

As was the custom of the day, wealthy and prominent parishioners were buried both inside and outside the church. Those buried outside would have their graves marked by tombstones and monuments; those buried on the inside would have a marker placed on the floor of the church. There are hundreds—some suggest several thousand—buried in the grounds around the church. Three of our country's founding fathers—George Washington, Thomas Jefferson, and Patrick Henry—attended Bruton Parish Church as members of the Virginia legislature, when it was in session. Members of the Virginia House of Burgesses, in support of the city of Boston, participated in a day of fasting, humiliation, and prayer when the British navy closed Boston's port in 1774. They all marched to Bruton Parish Church in solemn protest as the prewar tensions continued to rise. Soon after, two events created a period for the church where it fell into disrepair and lost the bulk of its members: the Virginia legislature ended tax support of the Anglican church (1776), and Thomas Jefferson, governor of Virginia at the time, ordered the capital to be moved to Richmond (1780). In fact, the moving of the capital to Richmond is what put the city of Williamsburg out of the limelight and back to its original status as a small town in a rural farming community. For a brief period in the Civil War, Williamsburg came back into the spotlight in the Battle of Williamsburg in May of 1862. After that battle, Bruton served as a hospital for wounded Confederate soldiers. It was not until the year 1939 that this old church was restored to the authentic splendor that it enjoyed during its per-Revolutionary War days when Williamsburg was the capital of England's largest colony in North America.

So that's just a little bit of the church's history; and on a walk down the Duke of Gloucester Street from Merchant's Square, it is one of the first buildings to really catch your eye.

Narrative, Insights & Introspection

As I mentioned in the preface, I decided to do a series of night photographs to capture paranormal activity in and around Williamsburg, and this happened to be the first building that I came upon to photograph—but on my second visit. My first attempt was on a cold winter's night, and the wind chill encouraged me to keep my hands in my pockets as much as possible— gloves just do not work on all of the buttons and the wheel that all require constant attention when adjusting the camera for a particular shot! There were lots of low-hanging, spirited white clouds with just a touch of blush from the city lights that seemed to be in a rush to get wherever they were going. It was a dramatic sky, and church had just let out, so all the lights were still on inside. I thought that this was a great photograph; the icing on the cake would be to have some sort of apparition show up on set. For the next couple of hours I traipsed through Williamsburg, photographing eighteenth-century houses, cold and alone, just waiting and hoping to find something—anything—out of the realm of normal. But my first set of photographs was

Figure 1: Here is the church's southeast side, still lit up after a service. (Dramatic sky, but no evidence of the paranormal here.)

a bust all the way around Williamsburg. It was a very dramatic series of night photographs of the buildings with billowing white clouds and a dark blue sky, but that wasn't what I was looking for. I went home, cold and discouraged, thinking that I was just wasting my time.

It was another month and a half before I decided to try again, the frigid cold and the failure of the first attempt holding me back. Not nearly as cold, I began at the Bruton Parish Church, drawn to it once again by the glow in the windows from the interior lights still on for an evening service that had just let out. After the flood of people and cars, I set up for a shot facing due north. To my surprise, when I looked at the image I captured, I saw this beautiful light formation hovering above the roof— success! It did not stay in one place, but moved about the roof area with each subsequent photo. I could not see it with the naked eye, but every photograph that I took; this light formation was somewhere on or hovering about the roof of the old church. Could it be one of the persons buried in the floor of the church, or perhaps in the tombs or monuments in the surrounding graveyard? Could it be one of the soldiers who was treated and died there during the Civil War? Could it be the spirit of Daniel Custis, first husband of Martha Custis (Washington), looking for his beloved wife—who was buried in northern Virginia with her second husband (George Washington) instead of next to him in the empty grave he bought right next to the church? Could it be one of the governors of Colonial Virginia, or perhaps even one of the rectors of the church, watching over and guarding their church from evil? No one knows for sure, but you can't deny this beautiful colored light apparition that hovers over the roof of this 300-year-old house of worship, no matter who or what you think it is.

Is There a Scientific Link Between Light and Life?

I was very pleased at my success, but at the same time I had this nagging doubt: Why didn't this creature that moved about the roof of the church look like the stereotypical Halloween

Figure 1a: In this later photograph, facing due north, I found my first example of a paranormal light—and it cannot be seen with the naked eye; it reminds me of a sentinel guarding the church. This photograph was taken about a month and a half after the first one, at a different angle, and the exposure was not as long (which is why you can't see any blue sky or clouds). A church service had let out about twenty minutes before this photo too, so all of the inside lights are still on. My paranormal odyssey began here, with this photograph.

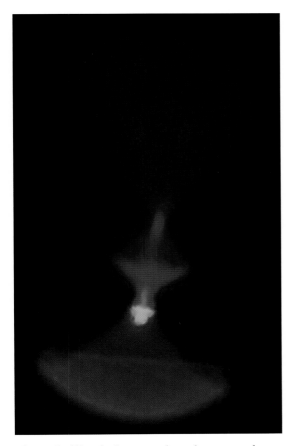

Figure 1b: Here is the same photo, but cropped so that all you see is the paranormal light formation.

ghost? This wasn't frightening; this looked like a piece of modern art juxtaposed against an eighteenth-century architectural relic. As I went around Colonial Williamsburg, I began to capture similar apparitions, with variations in color, size, and geometry. I looked over the Internet but found nothing like what I had captured— mostly just some semi-transparent small grey orbs. I wondered if there was any scientific evidence or proof about what I had captured, and that's when I discovered the work of Polish physicist Janusz Slawinski.

Slawinski opens his paper with this statement in his abstract.

Recent research into spontaneous radiations from living systems suggests a scientific foundation for the ancient association between light and life, and a biophysical hypothesis of the conscious self that could survive death of the body. All living organisms emit low-intensity light; at the time of death, that radiation is ten to 1,000 times stronger than that emitted under normal conditions.[1]

The physicist lays the foundation for a surprising conclusion by first stating that all living organisms, from man down to the very smallest one-celled creatures, create an electromagnetic field. Slawinski cites research proving that basic biological functions, such as respiration, cell reproduction, thought, and movement initiate electromagnetic fields. In fact, part of the field that surrounds an organism extends beyond the physical body, formulating what some call an electromagnetic aura (keep in mind that light is a part of the electromagnetic spectrum).

Living organisms emit light (photons) not at random, but in a sequence indicating a temporal order that may imply some validity to the elec-tromagnetic theory of life hypothesized by other scientific researchers. The physicist is building a case for his postulation that we may not have a physical consciousness defined by the parameters of our brain, but an *electromagnetic conscious-ness,* fully capable of organizing inanimate mat-ter (our bodies) into an animated physical being. Modifications to this life force are made by our

Figure 1c: On another evening, I wondered if the "entity" would be there at dusk, when the sky was still blue. Here it is in electric blue, not quite as bright, and the other colors do not show up quite as well, but it's still there at about twenty minutes after the sunset. Notice that the light formation is not on the roof this time, but hovering about ten or fifteen feet above it!

Figure 1d: Here is the same photograph as Figure 1c, but cropped so that you just see the apparition. Is it the same apparition? What do you think?

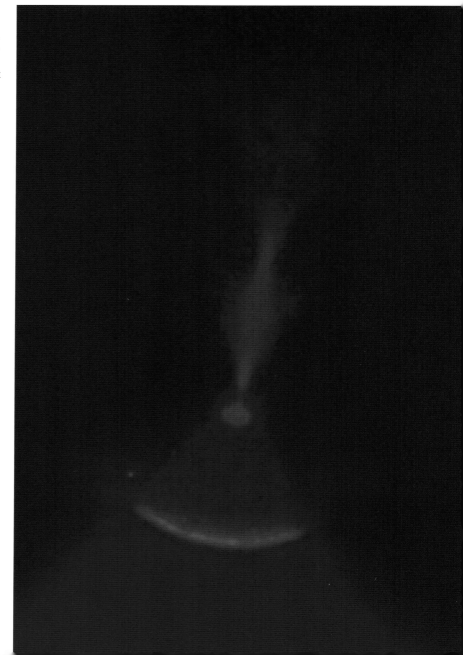

genetics and our environment, essentially making us the individuals that we are.

This electromagnetic consciousness dwells within our physical bodies, but upon death, this life force separates from our bodies at the speed of light—the *death flash*: hence the measured photo emission that can be up to 1,000 times greater than our normal rate. (This part of the hypothesis has been proven through research.)

Now keep in mind that Slawinski is a physicist for this next part, because although it's profound, it's crucial to explain a few things about what I've photographed: if you couple this idea of a separate, electromagnetic consciousness with Einstein's special theory of relativity, some questions can be answered. Because the being (the ghost) is no longer physical upon death but an electromagnetic intelligence, it exists outside the parameters (limitations) of both time and space—it is timeless, it exists, from our physical perspectives, forever. According to Einstein's theory, the ghosts would be separate from our existence on earth (within the space time continuum), and separated by "that impenetrable barrier, the speed of light."[2]

So we, the physical beings, are on a different plane of existence from the ghosts, making open communication impossible. But wait; some ghosts have learned to cross that barrier— or is it the humans? Slawinski thinks that breaking that barrier can be done with the psychic ability to project our consciousness out of body into the realm (plane or continuum of no space and no time) of the ghosts.

If I could go one step further, based on the photographic evidence I've accumulated, I would theorize that the shapes and colors of these creatures that I have captured are like an electromagnetic "fingerprint" of these entities or ghosts. As you will quickly find out, some of these electromagnetic consciousnesses (ghosts) have learned how to bend and shape light to re-create their former human likenesses, projecting light much like a hologram onto windows, sides of houses, and other curious locations you will see throughout this book. So now that you are armed with scientific facts and theories explaining the possibilities of paranormal existence, you may find it easier to mentally process some of the apparitions that you will see—ranging from the beautiful to the bizarre, from innocuous to evil—and accept this alternate reality that I'm about to show you.

Endnotes

1. Jansz Slawinski, "Electromagnetic Radiation and the Afterlife, New Dualism Archive" (1987, Accessed March 25, 2015), PDF document available online: http://www.newdualism.org.
2. Ibid.

CHAPTER TWO

St. George Tucker House

The Beautiful and the Bizarre

History

A man named William Levingston built the first theater in America, and he also built a home for himself in 1716. St. George Tucker, a man whose first name was taken from the patron saint of England, purchased the home and three lots in 1788 and promptly moved the whole house to a new site on Nicholson Street. Additions were made to the original structure to accommodate Tucker's growing family: he ended up with nine children, and five stepchildren from two marriages. Among Tucker's notable accomplishments: he was a lawyer, Revolutionary War militia officer, judge, and legal scholar and writer. As a legal scholar and writer, one of his notable achievements was to edit *Blackstone's Commentaries on the Laws of England* (Philadelphia, 1803), and apply them to the context of American democracy. He constructed Williamsburg's first bathroom in an outbuilding that once housed his dairy. Another thing Tucker's house is famous for is that in 1842 it was the site of the first Christmas tree erected in America: William & Mary Professor Charles F. E. Minnigerode, a friend of one of Tucker's sons and a political refugee from a German principality, put up a tree for the enjoyment of Tucker's grandchildren. This original home was restored by Colonial Williamsburg in 1931. Although not one of the official ghost stories of Williamsburg, some people have claimed to see a pale, older lady dressed in black, with her hair in a bun and shawl over her shoulders standing in front of the Tucker house.

Narrative, Insights, & Introspection

Having tried a few photographs at the George Wythe home, one of the so-called haunted houses in Colonial Williamsburg, with nothing paranormal showing up that evening (after quite a few photos!), I tried this home with the hope of better results. I was amazed at what I found; it was a similarly shaped apparition to the one on the Bruton Parish Church, but much taller. A second time I photographed the house, several months later, an interesting thing happened. I had taken several photos and got nothing, when a group of middle school age children started coming down the street. They were laughing and carrying on rather loudly for an evening in Colonial Williamsburg, and so before they arrived I decided to take several more photos. The first try, the apparition appeared at ground level, and it was barely there. The second try, the apparition came in a little clearer, as if it was gaining strength—or waking up, and it was at the second-floor level. The third take, it had risen to the roof of the home, and it was at its brightest. Evidently, the apparition was at ground level and barely visible when the noise from the children roused it, and it rose to the rooftop of the building to observe the entourage coming down the street. I went to the home several months later to see if I could catch images that were similar: There were differences between the apparition's appearance each time I photographed it. Can these apparitions change their appearance at will; are they the real shape-shifters? Compare the photos yourself—is it the same apparition?

Another question that I can't help asking is, Do these apparitions need to go into periods of inactivity, or is their activity perhaps out of boredom? Do they shut down their light and go into a kind of sleep? Or do they go into another dimension of existence? Do they even need sleep? It makes logical sense that a creature, whether it is made up of matter or energy, needs time to replenish itself. Do they feed off anything? What are their requirements for sustaining life? Then again, it is possible that I am equating human needs, like food and sleep, to a creature that is obviously not made up of flesh and blood. All of these questions course through my mind as I watch this apparition that my camera sees but I cannot move about the roof of this eighteenth-century house. I can see it moving closer to me as it must be curious about what I am doing there. I, for my part, am completely oblivious to psychic phenomena and probably would not be aware if one of these apparitions stood right in front of me.

Besides the question of sleep, hibernation, or just inactivity is something that seemed obvious: this apparition was, for lack of a better word, "awakened" by the voices of children laughing and joking around. They are social creatures! They evidently are activated by the human voice, and although they have no mouth or voice box with which to speak, they obviously can hear and react to sounds—suggesting that they are alive and intelligent.

The St. George Tucker apparition is one that I can always rely on to be there. I have returned frequently because it never disappoints. The ghosts of other eighteenth century homes may be elusive and difficult to capture, but this apparition is like "Old Faithful." I have caught it in many forms, dressed in many colors, and taking on many shapes, but it is always there. As you will see later on in this book, there are homes that have faces that are ghostly white, or blood red, or that have the likeness of someone from the past, or that have distorted features that would frighten most people—but at the St. George Tucker House, like the Bruton Parish Church, I can always see what reminds me of an angel of light.

After my second success at capturing these apparitions, it was apparent that the Bruton Parish Church was no fluke: Using the right camera, with the right settings and techniques, I can capture what people have been trying to prove or disprove for years—ghosts really exist! I see programs on television where they get a little glitch or shadow on video and they seem elated. I can take real photographs, with great detail and color of these apparitions—we now have real evidence of life forms all around us that we cannot see or hear—but now we know they are really there! Do you believe in ghosts now? Read on, because I have lots more proof!

Figure 1: Here is the photo from my first visit to the St. George Tucker house, showing an elegant apparition giving off several different colors of light.

Figure 2: This photo is from my second visit to the St. George Tucker house with the "awakened" apparition rising up to the roof from the ground. Although it looks like two apparitions, it moved as one. You will see this throughout this book—these light apparitions that are overhead houses and building are in two parts, with an invisible connection in between.

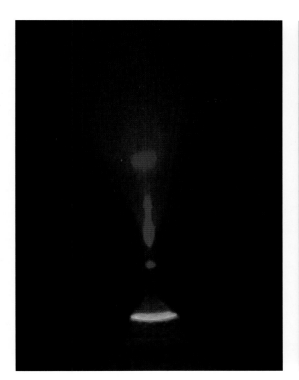

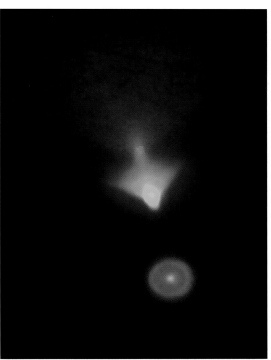

Here is the cropped photo of Figure 1 showing just the apparition; I think that this is my favorite because of the elegant shape and beautiful colors.

I included a photo taken just a few seconds (Figure 2) later to show how quickly these apparitions can alter their appearance. Although it moved as one apparition, it has the appearance of two!

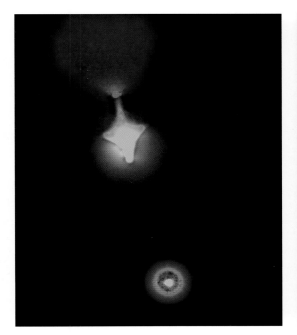

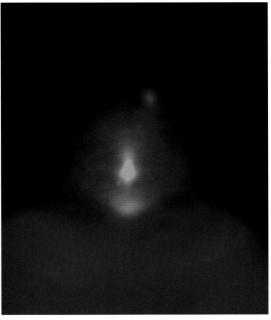

Here is the cropped version of Figure 2. Is it the same apparition as the first one? It appears to be completely different—perhaps there are two spirits that guard this house at night, or perhaps they are shape-shifters.

Here is another version of the St. George Tucker apparition taken a few days later—changing again; some say that you can see a face in this apparition.

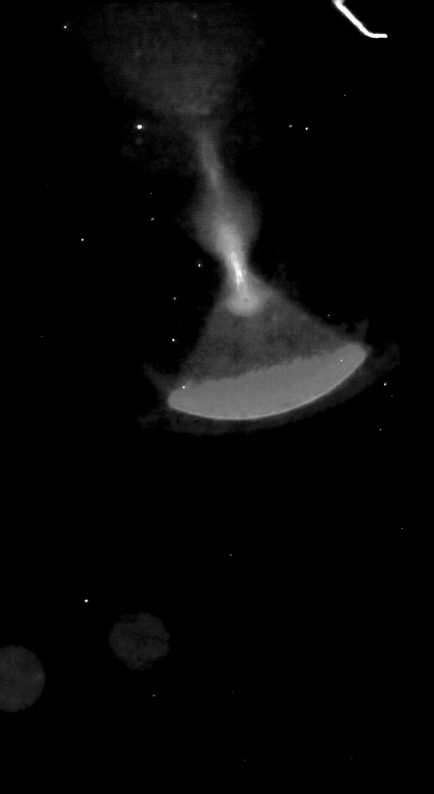

Another cropped photograph from the St. George
Tucker House; this time not only showing a beautiful
apparition, but also two orbs (below) and a streak of
white light (at the top—another apparition—they
move incredibly fast!).

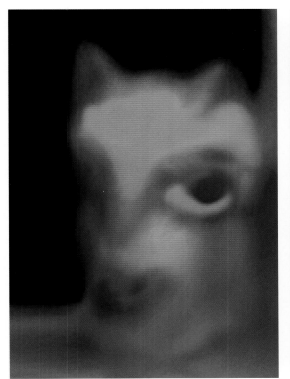

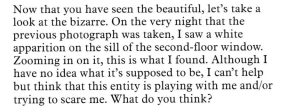

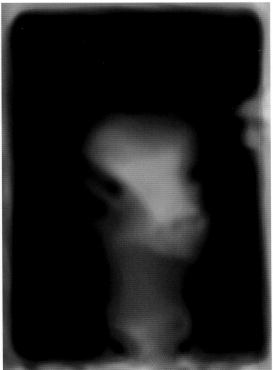

Now that you have seen the beautiful, let's take a look at the bizarre. On the very night that the previous photograph was taken, I saw a white apparition on the sill of the second-floor window. Zooming in on it, this is what I found. Although I have no idea what it's supposed to be, I can't help but think that this entity is playing with me and/or trying to scare me. What do you think?

A similar apparition appeared in another upstairs window, although this one appears as possibly two apparitions—a second apparition stacking on top of the first, with possibly a third making a mush smaller appearance as it peeks around the corner of the window.

CHAPTER THREE

Roscow Cole House

The Ghost of Christmas Present

History

The Roscow Cole house is an original eighteenth-century brick home built sometime between 1738 and 1750 to replace a rundown structure built in 1716. The building housed a plethora of businesses and tradesmen, including a gunsmith, tailors (one was named James Taylor), a clock and watchmaker, a wig-maker, a doctor with his own pharmacy (called an apothecary), a barber-surgeon, storekeepers, a teacher, and two dentists. Of interest to most people is that one of the dentists (Dr. John Baker) worked on George Washington's smile (have you ever seen a painting of George smiling?). The house was obviously a prime location for a business—it was right on the Market Square. In the days before supermarkets and refrigerators, every town would have an outdoor market. Farmers and fishermen would come in daily to set up stands and sell their produce, dairy products, or seafood. That meant that everyone in Williamsburg would have to go to the market every day to purchase the items needed for their meals for that day. So this property, facing the market area, was a prime location for just about any kind of business, and as you can tell, just about any type of businessman was willing to give this site a try.

As for the apparition that makes its home here, a former Colonial Williamsburg employee told me of a broken-hearted man who once lived here. His name was William Roscoe, and he was to marry a very independent, wealthy and beautiful young woman named Sarah Harrison. Young William, in school at the College of William and Mary, was himself looking towards a lucrative career as a lawyer. Although suitors were many and the competition stiff for Sarah, William won Sarah's heart (for the time being) and their engagement was announced. He and young Sarah actually had a marriage contract (common practice) that Sarah signed, stating that she would marry no other, and it was unheard of to break such a binding piece of paper in the eighteenth century. Nevertheless, impetuous Sarah did—much to the embarrassment of her family—and the wealthy and influential Harrison family was powerless to stop it. What was even more scandalous was fickle Sarah fell head-over-heels in love with a man almost twice her age just three weeks after the contract was signed. Young seventeen-year-old Sarah was love-struck by the founder of the College of William and Mary and rector of the Bruton Parish Church: The Reverend James Blair, thirty-one at the time. Sarah broke her word and her contract with the young lawyer-in-training and married the charismatic James Blair.

Young William is said to have died of a broken heart within these walls; his secret hidden within the unwritten history of this brick home, and his apparition may be the one that appears overhead or locked inside a window—peering out at all of the Christmases he could have had with his beautiful Sarah.

Narrative, Insights & Introspection

One evening during the Christmas season, I came down with a few friends to see the Fife and Drum Corps perform, and hear a choir singing eighteenth-century Christmas songs. The choir stood on the steps of the courthouse of 1770, with locals and tourists gathered all around to watch and sing, complete with baskets of burning wood all around the perimeter to provide light and warmth to all the participants on this December evening. After photographing all of the activities, I got bored and began to look around: I was drawn to a house that faces the western side of the courthouse. I quickly discovered an electric blue apparition that was burning brightly on the roof. It was much smaller than either the apparition at the Bruton Parish Church or the one at the St. George Tucker House, and it only gave off the electric blue-colored light. During my photo session at the house, the first photograph showed the apparition on the roof and at an angle going out to the left—it was watching the activities at the courthouse! These apparitions are drawn to people, noise, and light.

As I took photos of the house, the ghost remained on the roof, as close as possible to the festivities—it must have been listening and observing the Christmas holiday celebration. Once the Christmas program at the courthouse of 1770 concluded, I saw something strange happen through the eye of my camera: it was a very cold night, causing the crowd to disperse immediately, and the unfed baskets of fire began to die quickly. In the subsequent photos, the apparition began to rise up into the sky, until it finally disappeared from view. Obviously the entity was attracted to all the activity going on next door in the Christmas present, and once it was over, it left the scene. (The second photo shows the entity hovering over the Roscow Cole house.) The apparition's ascension into the sky gives rise to the question, where does it go? Does it go up to heaven (wherever or whatever that is)? How long does it leave the home before it comes back? Why does it leave, and more importantly why does it come back? I have subsequently found the apparition back at the home, and of course I wonder what holds it there? Does it choose to stay there or is it trapped? What do you think? Is the ghost of Christmas present the broken-hearted young lover who was spurned so long ago? Does he watch and reminisce about all of the Christmases he could have had with his beautiful bride—had she actually married him?

Figure 3: Here is the scene next door to the Roscow-Cole House at the Courthouse of 1770, where crowds have gathered to see the Fife and Drum Corps and sing eighteenth-century Christmas carols.

Figure 3a: Here is the first photograph of the Roscow-Cole House; notice in this one that the apparition is on the roof of the home, and is almost all blue.

Figure 3c: Here is the second photograph of the Roscow-Cole house; notice in this one that the apparition is hovering over the roof of the home and is in the process of ascending up into the sky. (A few minutes and several photos later, the paranormal light was completely out of sight.)

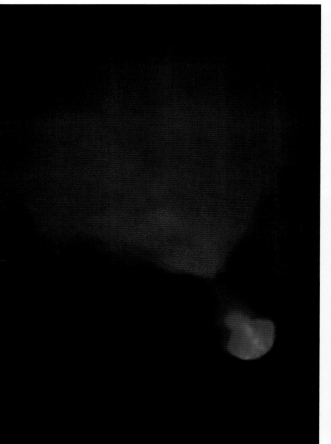

Figure 3b: Here is the cropped photo showing just the apparition.

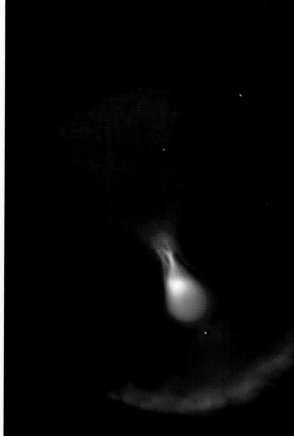

Figure 3d: Here is the cropped photo, showing just the apparition as it begins to ascend into the sky; it will disappear in just a few minutes (and several photos later).

The Gap-Mouthed Ghosts

In his 1843 novella *A Christmas Carol*, Charles Dickens wrote a description of the ghost of Jacob Marley, a victim in the afterlife to his own greed and avarice. When Marley's ghost comes to visit his former partner Ebenezer Scrooge, Dickens gave a curious detail about the phantom moneychanger:

> Though he looked the phantom through and through, and saw it standing before him; though he felt the chilling influence of its death-cold eyes; and marked the very texture of the folded kerchief bound about its head and chin, which wrapper he had not observed before: he was still incredulous, and fought against his senses.[3]

The thing I want you to take note of is *the folded kerchief bound about its head and chin.* Note what happens when the ghost removes the kerchief:

> At this the spirit raised a frightful cry, and shook its chain with such a dismal and appalling noise, that Scrooge held on tight to his chair, to save himself from falling in a swoon. But how much greater was his horror, when the phantom taking off the bandage round its head, as if it were too warm to wear indoors, its lower jaw dropped down upon its breast![4]

Notice that the ghost uses a handkerchief to hold his mouth closed, and when he removes it, the ghost's jaw drops open—all the way to his chest. Take a look at the ghost on this page, possibly a young man from the eighteenth century; could it be William Roscoe? This is the first of many photos you will see in this book series of a phantom with its mouth inexplicably gaping open. No, not all the way to the chest, but I imagine Dickens took a little creative license. But this detail in Dickens' description makes me think that sometime in his life Dickens had a personal experience with a gap-mouthed ghost. I find it curious to discover so many apparitions that actually show their mouths gaping open, and that this writer included this wraith characteristic in

Figure 3e: One of the faces that I found looking through the blinds at the Roscow Cole House.

his seminal Christmas ghost story. Did he have a sixth sense? Before he wrote this Christmas classic, did Dickens see dead people?

I had long-finished both this chapter and the book when I described the anomaly of the gap-mouthed ghosts to a friend of mine, who is a registered nurse. She immediately came up with an explanation that made sense to me that only a doctor or nurse would know: A lot of times when someone dies their mouth opens as the muscles to the jaw relax—she would have to close the mouth. But if the ghost departs from the body with the mouth open, perhaps that makes an imprint on its memory—and how it will project the image of itself to others.

Endnotes

3, Charles Dickens, *A Christmas Carol*, (London, England: Chapman & Hall, 1843).

4. Ibid.

CHAPTER FOUR

Peyton Randolph House

Something Wicked This Way Haunts

History

The Peyton Randolph house's (named after its most famous owner) original west wing was built in 1715 by William Robertson and purchased in 1721 by Sir John Randolph, who had the distinction of being the only colonial Virginian to be knighted. John Randolph was a lawyer who graduated from the College of William and Mary; he later became a prominent attorney, a member of the Virginia House of Burgesses, and the attorney general for the colony of Virginia. He bought the lot next to his home and constructed a second house on the property. Sir John died in 1737 and was buried beneath the floor of the Wren building at the College of William and Mary. In 1859, fire gutted the Wren building (its outer walls remained standing), and the burial vaults were disturbed. A physician who examined the tomb of John Randolph discovered a second body in the grave—and no one knows who the second person is or how the body got there. Was the second body placed in the tomb at the time of John Randolph's death, or was the tomb opened at a later time to place the unidentified body inside? Could this have anything to do with the haunting at the Randolph home? One could only speculate.

When his father died, the family home and the house next door were willed to John's son Peyton Randolph (his mother would possess the home till Peyton reached the age of twenty-four), who built a two-story structure between the two houses to make one large house. Peyton had quite a few of the same accomplishments that his father had: he studied law at the College of William and Mary; he became attorney general of Virginia, and he was a member of the Virginia House of Burgesses (he would become Speaker of the House). In addition, he presided over the first (1774) Continental Congress. He was the first man to be called "the father of our country," and many had no doubt that he would be our country's first president! He died of a stroke in Philadelphia in 1775, and subsequently, the title was bestowed on George Washington. Peyton's wife would live out her remaining days in the house—they did not have children. Although the Randolphs were colonial Virginia's first family in wealth and importance, the fledgling country soon forgot about them. His cousin, Thomas Jefferson, purchased Peyton Randolph's book collection after Peyton's wife, Betty, died in 1783. Jefferson would later sell his collection of books (including Peyton Randolph's books) to the Library of Congress; to this day, historians regularly consult Peyton's bound records of early Virginia history. General Washington, General Lafayette, and General Rochambeau were some of the noted and welcome guests to have dined and/or stayed in the house—but you are probably interested in the unwelcome guests—or ghosts.

After 1783, the house was sold at an auction and passed through different owners until Colonial Williamsburg bought and restored the home (in 1940 and further restoration in 1968) to its colonial splendor. The red color the home is painted today is indicative of the family's wealth that lived there; that particular color could only be afforded by the wealthy (it was a labor-intensive pigment that required the makers to capture and grind up tens of thousands of cochineal beetles).

Narrative & Insights on the Haunting

According to Colonial Williamsburg employees, the Peyton Randolph house is the most haunted house in all of Williamsburg (unofficially). The Colonial Williamsburg Foundation wants to be identified with history, and not paranormal activity, so you will never hear a word from official channels or in advertisements about the hauntings—although Colonial Williamsburg does run a "Ghost Tour." But the Peyton Randolph house is home to a plethora of paranormal activity, including heavy footsteps, the sounds of breaking glass (no glass is ever broken), and the occasional appearance of an angry man dressed in colonial attire. There has also been the appearance of a nervous old woman dressed in colonial sleeping attire when people actually lived in the home—but no one stays in the home now (Colonial Williamsburg rents some of its homes out to employees; other homes, like the St. George Tucker house, are used to give special accommodations to generous donors to the foundation). The Colonial Williamsburg Foundation doesn't like to acknowledge that their buildings are haunted, but they are smart enough not to rent this building out to an employee or let a wealthy donor stay overnight. (They just might take back their donation, if they even make it through the night!)

By far, the most frequent complaint of the interpreters who work at the Peyton Randolph house is the sensation of being pushed down the stairs by an unseen spirit. It seems to happen to only the employees, and not the tourists. Some current and former employees (who are even willing to talk about it) speculate that the ghost only shoves people who dress in colonial attire (the interpreters) and not the tourists because its anger is directed towards the people

of its time. However, I do know of a cleaning woman who was not dressed in eighteenth-century clothing who felt two hands on her shoulders that attempted to push her down the stairs. Some have gone so far as to speculate that the ghost is a runaway female African-American slave named Eve who was captured and returned to the house. It was said that she suffered a severe beating for escaping; could she be responsible for the malevolent activity in the house? There are many other ghost stories that go with the Randolph house; L.B. Taylor Jr. documented them in his book *The Ghosts of Williamsburg . . . and Nearby Environs.* There have been quite a few deaths at the house, several that were suicides, and some employees have expressed feelings of discomfort or sense an evil presence in the home. Add all of the deaths together and couple that with the mysterious, unidentified body found in Sir John Randolph's tomb, and you have the perfect recipe for paranormal activity. Just this past summer, two groups of between twenty and twenty-five people on a ghost tour, overheard a loud crashing noise as they listened to their guides explain the paranormal activity. The crashing noise was so loud they heard it from across the street of the house, and it set off motion detectors in the home. Colonial Williamsburg's security team immediately responded to the alarm—and do you know what they found? Nothing broken, nothing moved, nothing out of place . . . what made the crashing sounds?

There are a couple interesting stories about the house that I heard firsthand from Colonial Williamsburg employees. The first is about a security guard who answered the motion detector alarm indicating that someone was in the house (a few years ago). He unlocked the door and went inside to do a walkthrough of the whole house. Finding nothing on the first floor or the second, he went down to the basement to take a look down there, because he thought he heard someone calling for help. The basement was clear, but when he went to leave, he found himself locked in. He had a key for every door, but he could not open the lock. He tried to open the door calmly at first, and after hearing the footsteps and crashing sounds that the house is known for, began to use force. He bent the key—but the door would not open. The next morning security found him huddled in the corner of the basement; after he gave up trying to unlock the door, he went back to the interior of the room, where he felt paralyzed and could not move (whether it was from fear or from a temporary physical condition, no one knows for sure). Offering no detailed explanation, he handed his gun and badge to the security team that found him and quit on the spot. "I will never set foot on Colonial Williamsburg property again!" he exclaimed as he left.

A tour guide that I know was giving a ghost tour outside the Peyton Randolph House and across the street in the market square (the lawn area surrounding the courthouse of 1770, used by local farmers and fishermen to sell their produce, dairy products, and seafood). She was explaining several of the stories that L.B. Taylor had written in his book, after which one member of the group asked her what story she liked the best. She immediately responded that she liked the story associated with the George Wythe House, and before she could say another word, she was shoved to the ground by an unknown force. She had a group of twenty-five people, who all bore witness that this was not just a bump, but a forceful shove from behind that pushed her face-first into the ground. Evidently the creature or spirit there thinks that the Peyton Randolph House has the best ghost story of all!

So far you have seen apparitions that have been colorful and displaying beautiful, abstract geometric shapes. But for some reason, at the Peyton Randolph house, you only see either "orbs" (small circular-shaped lights that only show up as a grey color) or reflections in the windows that so eerily reflect the surrounding street lamps. Does that have something to do with the fact that people who have experienced the home's paranormal activity feel that there is an "evil" presence within the house? So far you have seen apparitions with beautiful forms and colors; does the color, size, and shape of the apparition reveal whether it is good or evil? It's something to think about . . .

The Bruton Parish Church was the first place I captured an apparition, but at "Williamsburg's most haunted," I captured my first wraith that resembled a human face. In one of the windows on the bottom left side of the Peyton Randolph House, in one of the windowpanes, occupying the top half of the pane, I discovered the very first ghost *face* that I'd found anywhere, but I was disappointed because the bottom of the man's face looked very dark and distorted; you could not distinguish his mouth or the bottom of his nose. The elation that I actually captured a recognizable face was coupled with the frustration that it was only a partial visage—that is until I learned the background of this entity from a former Colonial Williamsburg employee: a man committed suicide in this very room by putting a gun to his mouth—and then it made perfect sense! No wonder that I could not tell what the bottom of the ghost's face looked like—he had blown it away with a gun! As you will see by the paranormal occupants, the Peyton Randolph House more than lives up to its reputation!

Figure 4: Here is the Peyton Randolph House surrounded by grey "orbs"; some refer to this as an orb blizzard. I don't know if they all stay here or if they came from other parts of Williamsburg to get their picture taken. No beautiful colors, no elegant shapes, just grey—and in some cases misshapen—orbs. Again, does the color, size, and shape of an apparition reveal whether it's good or evil? Look closely— some are very faint! On this night, I had the help of a nearly full moon to illuminate this very dark house.

Figure 4a: The Governor's Palace is full of light reflections—but none of them have any apparitions when you examine them closely.

Figure 4b: Now look at what can be seen in the windows of the Peyton Randolph House! This is a photo of the ominous-looking Peyton Randolph house on a darker, moonless night; unofficially it's the most haunted house in all of Colonial Williamsburg. The windows are reflecting several street lanterns along the streets by the house; otherwise, the house is very dark (I used the headlights from my car to illuminate it)—and perhaps indicative of the darkness belonging to the entity or entities that occupy the house.

Figure 4c: In one of the windows on the bottom left side of the Peyton Randolph House, in one of the windowpanes occupying the top half of the pane, I discovered this apparition. It was the very first ghost face that I'd found anywhere, but I was disappointed because the bottom of the man's face looked very dark and distorted; you could not distinguish his mouth or the bottom of his nose. Then I learned that a man committed suicide in this very room by putting a gun to his mouth—then it made perfect sense!

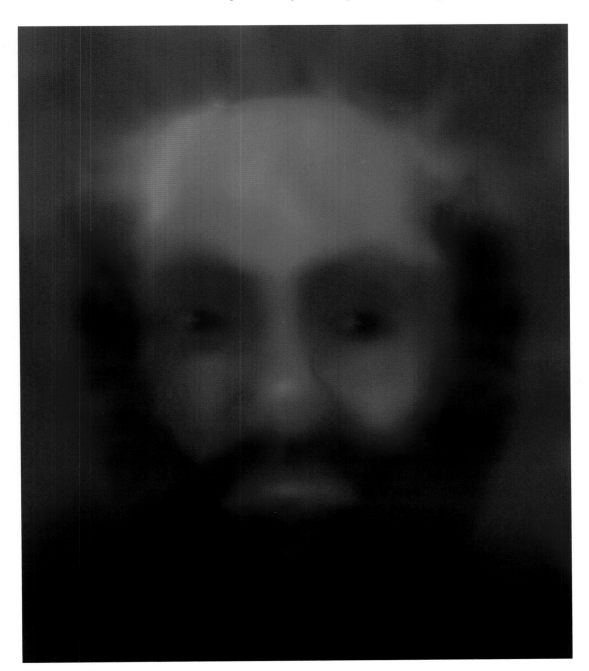

Figure 4d: I found quite a few shapes in the windows that resembled skulls, but an objective person might say the shapes were a little ambiguous, so I left them out. But this cropped photo with a boost of the contrast revealed what appears to be a bald man with a beard; whether he resembles any drawings or paintings of the house's previous occupants I do not know. Men in the eighteenth century were clean-shaven; this gentleman looks like he would be from the nineteenth century—probably around the Civil War era.

Now watch how the photo is cropped to three windows (crop #1), then to one window, then to one windowpane to show the face of some unknown person.

Crop #2: (Can you see the face yet?)

Crop #3

Another odd combination that seems to be par for the Peyton Randolph House: a face in one windowpane and an over-sized eye in another. The eye is not really shaped like a human eye, but perfectly round—more like an animal's. But then most animals do not show this much white in the eye—that's unlike any animal I've seen. What animal could this eye belong to?

In one of the stories about the Peyton Randolph House, a young boy fell out of a tree in the backyard. He would later die inside the house in an upstairs bedroom. I don't know if this is the same boy, but I did find him looking out of a downstairs window (keep in mind that young boys wore their hair long then). Other children from the Peachy family, who purchased the home in 1824, also perished in the home from diseases. One little girl fell down the stairs to her death—was she pushed by the entity? Could this be her?

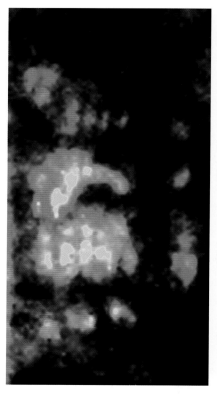

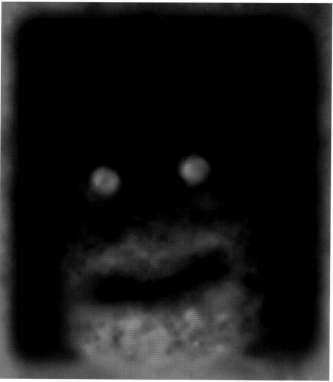

An example of the ambiguous: As I said before, there are some windowpanes that had something ambiguous in them; I wonder if it's just a coincidence of light and reflection in the window, but I will leave you to be the judge. For the above figure on the left, I've had many different interpretations: the face of a demon, the face of an African-American woman slave—perhaps Eve, the slave that escaped and was recaptured? (turned sideways, with a cap and a long dress, perhaps with a shawl), a little girl (on the right, towards the bottom), a heavy-set man with a bushy beard (top left), and multiple faces of demons or ghosts. So make your own interpretation, or chalk it up as an abstract reflection of light; above is a second example.

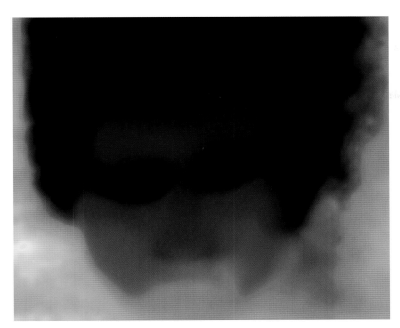

This is another ambiguous apparition on the outside of one of the windowpanes of the Peyton Randolph House; (he, she, it?) looks like another unpleasant character. Some think that this is Eve. What do you think?

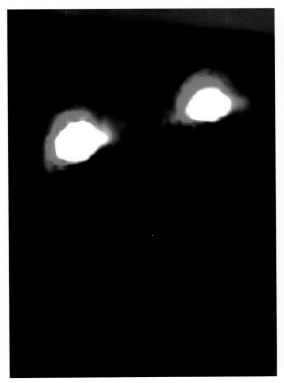

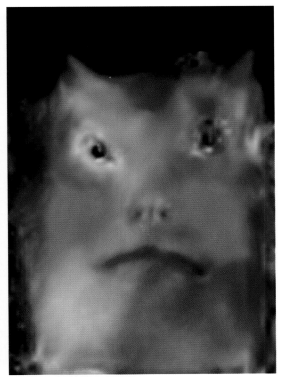

This photo is the one that I talked about in the introduction: My wife, the reluctant psychic, could actually see this pair of glowing eyes staring at her from an upstairs window—I could not. She immediately wanted to leave, explaining that this was not a good place. When I asked her what she'd seen, she said with a smirk, "You're the one who claims he can photograph ghosts. You tell me!" I asked her if at the very least she could point out where "it" was, and this is the photo I took. She has never doubted me since . . .

This last close-up of the Peyton Randolph House kind of sums up the presence inside, and it reminds me of the title of a book by Ray Bradbury: *Something Wicked This Way Comes*. Can you see a smaller eye coming out of the pupil of the eye on the right? This creature looks more like an alien or an animal rather than a human!

CHAPTER FIVE

Public Jail (Gaol)

13 Men in Dead Men's Coffins

History

When the capital of Virginia was moved from Jamestown to Williamsburg in 1699, the General Assembly ordered that a public jail (the word used in colonial times was *gaol*, an old word from Northern France that is pronounced the same way as the current word—jail) be built. Two cells were completed by 1704, with strong timbers laid underneath to prevent anyone from tunneling out of confinement. Unlike brick buildings today, the walls on the jail (as well as other colonial buildings) were substantial—more than just a one-brick façade.

In the eighteenth century, jail was not the punishment; jail was designed just to hold the accused until the trial (usually not more than three months, because court was held four times per year). Punishments for crimes were corporal: branding, whipping, hanging, time in the pillory or stocks, although a first time criminal may be shown mercy and just fined. After two additional cells were added in 1711, debtors began to be held in the gaol for twenty days at the public's expense. Any time after twenty days the creditors had to pay to keep the prisoner. In times of war (both the Revolutionary and the Civil Wars), one could find that the gaol's occupants could be spies, prisoners of war, deserters, and traitors. The year 1722 saw another expansion to the jail: the jail-keeper's quarters were expanded, a courtyard was added, and the total number of jail cells had increased to eight. When the capital moved from Williamsburg to Richmond in 1780, the facility became a county jail until 1910. The building was restored in 1936 by Colonial Williamsburg.

Some of the more interesting occupants of the Williamsburg gaol were pirates, particularly the crew of Blackbeard the Pirate. In the late seventeenth and early eighteenth century, piracy was a problem for Virginia. Pirates menaced the Atlantic shipping lanes to England, and Blackbeard was a big player. He had actually bribed the governor of North Carolina, but the governor of Virginia wanted Blackbeard dead. He sent Lieutenant Robert Maynard in the British Naval sloop the *Ranger* to hunt down Blackbeard. Here was the problem: the boat had no canons, but Blackbeard's ship did—this was like David going up against Goliath. Like David, Maynard knew there was more than one way to take down a giant. Lieutenant Maynard tricked Blackbeard into believing that the pirates' artillery fire had disabled the ship and crew. Maynard's men hid in the ship's hold, and when Blackbeard boarded the vessel, they surrounded the pirates. Maynard himself was nearly killed by Blackbeard, but one of his crew was able to get a shot off to save him. It took five pistol shots and twenty wounds from swords to finally take Blackbeard down; he was beheaded and his head placed on a pike at the confluence of the James River and Hampton River (or Creek, whichever you prefer) as a warning to all would-be pirates. As soon as their Goliath went down, the crew surrendered and were taken to the Williamsburg gaol to await trial. Blackbeard was never in the Williamsburg Jail—but his picture is! An original ink drawing of him still rests on the mantle in the entrance to the Williamsburg gaol; the drawing was used by the producers of the film series *Pirates of the Caribbean* to create the outfit for the character made famous by actor Johnny Depp—Captain Jack Sparrow. Of the fifteen men put on trial in Williamsburg for piracy, only two escaped the gallows. One of the men was Israel Hand, Blackbeard's first mate; he turned state's evidence on the other men in exchange for his freedom. He disappeared and turned up later in London, begging on the streets. He became the basis for the character Long John Silver in Robert Louis Stevenson's classic *Treasure Island.* (Stevenson actually has another character in the novel named Israel Hands; he is the ship's coxswain and a former gunner.)

The remaining thirteen men were tried, convicted of piracy, and sentenced to death. They were measured for their coffins, which arrived the day their sentence was carried out. Each man, on his execution day, was welded into shackles, forced to sit in his own coffin in an oxcart, and then paraded out the city of Williamsburg for all to see the consequences for a life of piracy. Then the oxcart drove the men to the gallows, where they were "turned off the cart," meaning after their neck was placed in the hangman's noose, the cart was pulled out from under them. They would each "dance the jig," meaning they would struggle and squirm as they were slowly suffocated by the noose before they finally died. Keep in mind that this was eighteenth-century entertainment, and a crowd would usually show up for any hanging—let alone the hanging of the crew of one of the most infamous pirates to ever stalk the coasts of Virginia and North Carolina. After the hanging, pirates were usually left by the water to rot for a while—to act as a deterrent against piracy to all of those who passed by. Sometimes the sound of the heavy oxcart carrying the doomed crew can still be heard on the streets of Williamsburg late at night; those who hear the noise and see nothing that could possibly make it are usually frightened; wouldn't you be?

The Williamsburg Gaol housed, besides the usual assortment of thieves and murderers, a mélange of others that you may not have thought of from a modern-day standpoint: runaway and/or disobedient slaves, Indians that were either guilty of breaking the law or conspiracy to revolt, people who were labeled insane (before the Public Hospital was built), debtors (you could not escape your debts by filing bankruptcy in the eighteenth century), and prisoners of war, including Henry Hamilton, given the well-deserved yet macabre nickname, "Hair-buyer." (Did you notice all of the alliteration? Henry Hair-buyer Hamilton) Hamilton was the British commander at Fort Detroit, who was captured in the frontier village of Vincennes (Indiana) by George Rogers Clark and his 175 Virginia militia men. Hamilton was vilified during the Revolutionary War for his policy of rewarding fighters from the Northwest Indian tribes for the scalps of Americans living on the frontier (at that time the Ohio Territory, considered part of the state of Virginia, including the area of these present-day states: Kentucky, parts of western Pennsylvania, Ohio, Indiana, Illinois, Michigan, Wisconsin, and Minnesota). Although Virginia Governor Patrick Henry had sent Clark on this mission, by the time Clark returned to Williamsburg with his infamous prisoner, it was thirteen days into the term of newly elected Governor Thomas Jefferson, who was outraged that a British officer guilty of such savagery expected "certain civilties" of him as he waited outside the Governor's Palace in the pouring rain. Jefferson ignored the savage nobleman, and Clark gladly escorted him to the Williamsburg Gaol, having him welded in heavy irons. Although not so much today, George Rogers Clark returned to Williamsburg a major Revolutionary War hero for the capture of the heinous Hamilton.[5] (By the way, George's brother became even more famous as part of the Lewis and Clark expedition.)

Hamilton had actively enlisted the help of indigenous tribes, supplied them with alcohol, knives for scalping, and enlisted white guides to make sure they attacked the right places on the frontier. The Indians were indiscriminate and would scalp women and children, particularly odious to Americans. Hamilton would pay the Indians a bounty for each scalp that they turned in, earning him the moniker "Hair-buyer." Hamilton, who even dressed and participated in Native American ceremonies before sending these war parties out, was complicit and guilty of murder in the eyes of the American people, particularly Thomas Jefferson. Even though Hamilton was both a British officer and member of the royalty, Jefferson had him put in heavy irons for most of his stay at the Williamsburg Gaol because he was guilty of heinous war crimes. Jefferson would later have the eighteen-pound irons removed and reluctantly released Hamilton—being so advised by his political peers, including Washington. They were certain that the mistreatment of a royal British officer would result in British retaliation to American prisoners-of-war that they held. In 1781, Hamilton was turned over to British forces in a prisoner-of-war exchange; he would later return to Canada as lieutenant governor and deputy governor of Quebec. He died on the island of Antigua in 1796,[6] but sometimes ghosts return to the site where they underwent trials, especially if they feel culpable and responsible in some way. He may be one of wraiths that is locked inside the jailhouse itself. I have captured several on camera, including two classic white Halloween-type ghosts, several large orbs, and a white, mist-like phantom taken in broad daylight. Does Hamilton feel any guilt for all the people, or perhaps just the women and children he had slaughtered—often still alive and terror stricken when their whole scalp was removed as a gruesome war trophy/bounty?

As if that were not enough to predict who might be haunting the jailhouse, another recent find drums up more possibilities as to who is perpetrating the haunting of the Williamsburg Gaol: eight bodies were found buried in the nearby surrounding ground; one was buried right under a foundation of the jail itself. Some websites state that the jail is simply haunted by two women (mentioned before that were thought to be insane) that can be heard in active conversation—I think there is a lot more to the hauntings than that!

Narrative & Introspection

Notice the photo of the back of the Gaol—thirteen orbs showed up over the building; just a coincidence? Although I knew the story of Blackbeard and his crew—I've told it many times—I found it a little eerie that thirteen orbs would show up over the jail the night that I photographed it. That evening I happened to be with a friend who is a reluctant psychic, and she told me about the face in the window of the jailor's house. According to some Colonial Williamsburg interpreters, the apparitions inside the jail are that of two women who were kept in the jailhouse because of insanity—they had not yet built the asylum. (The pirates were kept in the jail cells out back—attached to but not a part of the jailhouse where the jailor and his family resided. Upstairs cells inside the house were for women and the insane.) I could not see it, but when I moved in close to the window to take a photograph I felt a cold chill run down my spine. It was so cold that I knew it was not my imagination; something was close to me and draining the heat from my body. What makes it more frightening is the unknown factor; I'm not sure what these entities can and cannot do to a person. (The entity at the Peyton Randolph house has shoved people and given some an electric shock.) So far I have not been harmed; perhaps my fears are unwarranted and I'm guilty of watching too much television. I shall cautiously move on . . .

Figure 5: Here is a photograph of the front of the jail, showing the side that is the home of the jailer and his family. Nothing usually shows up when taking photos at this angle; the jail cells are on the western end of this building—but as you will see in Figure 5b, there are possibly two entities that have taken up residence here.

Figure 5a: The ink drawing of Blackbeard the Pirate inside the jail, and the inspiration for Johnny Depp's costume in the movie *Pirates of the Caribbean.*

Figure 5b: If you go to the other side of the jail, where they kept the prisoners, that's a different story. Do you remember the story of the thirteen men from Blackbeard's crew who were kept in this jail and were later hanged? Isn't it strange that in this photo, there are thirteen orbs hanging around the jail (gaol)? The largest and clearest orb is in the center of the roof. Look closely, some are very faint . . . but if you can't see them, hold on—they will be enhanced.

Figure 5c: Here is a cropped image showing the large orb with no enhancement—maybe four feet in diameter? Perhaps this is the leader of the jail's former inmates?

Except for the orb by the chimney, the rest of the orbs required a hefty boost in contrast to make them plainly visible. After seeing so many beautiful apparitions in other parts of this book—save for the Peyton Randolph House—doesn't it make you wonder? Is this some indicator of a human afterlife? And if it is, does how we live our lives affect how we look in the afterlife? Here you have dull grey, even misshapen circles of light hanging around an old jail and dark, frightening creatures in the windows of a dark house that nobody can live in, versus beautiful fountains of colored lights hanging over homes and a church.

Endnotes

5. Parke Rouse, "Henry Hair Buyer Hamilton," *Daily Press*, February 16, 1992, accessed September 27, 2015, http://articles.dailypress.com.

6. Bernard W. Sheehan, "The Famous Hair Buyer General: Henry Hamilton, George Rogers Clark, and the American Indian," accessed September 27, 2015, scholarworks.dlib.indiana.edu.

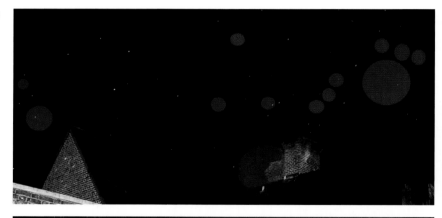

Figure 5d: Here is the top of the whole photograph showing all thirteen orbs (Blackbeard's crew?) with a healthy boost of contrast to make them visible. This is their last-known residence before they met the hangman!

Figure 5e: Here is another photograph of the back of the jail (gaol), but do you see what looks like a faint white light in the first floor window, bottom left pane? Wait till you see the close-up.

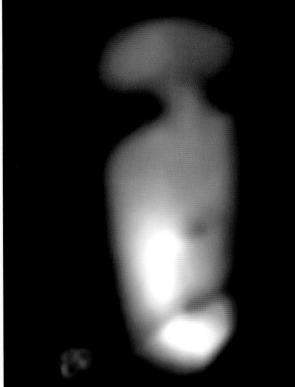

Figure 5f: Here is the cropped photograph of the lower left windowpane (with a healthy boost in contrast to bring out the apparition). I think this is the first time in this book that the photo is actually what most people expect a ghost to look like.

Figure 5g: A second photograph that I took immediately after the photo that had the face in the lower window had a second apparition in the left gable window on the roof. I have no idea what is on the bottom left.

Figure 5h: Unbeknownst to a Colonial Williamsburg interpreter and two young tourists who are listening to stories of the eighteenth-century jail, apparitions are all around them—perhaps they too want to hear what went on when they were alive. This photo has apparitional shapes that I had not seen before this point.

Figure 5i: Immediately after the Colonial Williamsburg interpreter, the young boy, and the young girl from Figure 5h left the room, I captured this mist-like apparition on the rather elaborate "throne"—eighteenth century slang for the toilet. It's not really a mist—it has nothing to do with water. It's low levels of white light are being emitted by one of the jail's ghosts.

CHAPTER SIX

Elkanah Deane House

A Real Ghost in the Machine

History

This home was built between 1720 and 1722; it's possible that John Robinson, speaker of the House of Burgesses and treasurer to the colony lived there until 1759, although there is no record to be found of him purchasing the property from the original owner, John Holloway. After Robinson's death, surgeon William Carter purchased the property and lived there until 1771. But the home was named after the man who purchased it in 1772—Virginia's premier coach-maker for the elite: Elkanah Deane.

Deane was an eighteenth-century coach-maker who lived in this home and set up his business on the four lots he purchased right off the Palace Green, building outbuildings to accommodate all of the various crafts involved in making some of the finest coaches in the colony of Virginia. In the mid-eighteenth century, Dublin, Ireland, became a coach-making center that rivaled the best that London had to offer. Deane served as an apprentice to one of the well-known coach-makers in Dublin, then worked as a journeyman there until he immigrated to New York City and built a shop there. He ran and managed the shop by himself, but later partnered with his brother, William. During the 1760s they had the most elaborate establishment of all the five coach-making shops in the city. The Deanes had many prominent customers, including Lord Dunmore, the royal governor of New York. In fact, Lord Dunmore was so pleased with Deane's work that he persuaded him to set up shop in Williamsburg when he

was appointed royal governor of Virginia in 1772. Elkanah left New York City to set up shop in Williamsburg, his first advertisement for the various types of coaches and carriages that he built appearing in the Williamsburg newspaper, the *Virginia Gazette*, in May of 1772. He prospered for several years in Williamsburg, serving elite customers like Thomas Nelson and George Washington. By 1775, Deane's business seemed to be suffering because people who he had extended credit to were not paying him, and he even put an advertisement in the paper asking his customers to pay him and warning new customers that he only worked on a cash basis. The business problems may have affected his health, because in October of that same year the paper reports the death of Elkanah Deane and the sale of his property.

Insights and a Ghost Story

I have taken quite a few photographs of this property, and there always seems to be one bright blue orb hovering around the small front porch over the house's main entrance off the Palace Green. Sometimes it's on the outside of the house, and sometimes it's on the inside of the central upstairs window. I have also noted a second apparition, similar to the one on the Roscow-Cole House, but not as bright, hovering over the rooftop every once in a while. It is not the same apparition as the other, because I have one photo that captures both the bright blue orb in the upstairs window and the apparition on the roof. If you notice there is a light on in the left downstairs window; I wonder if the person or persons there knew that two apparitions were there at the house, and one was right upstairs. They say that ghosts cannot move on because they have unfinished business; perhaps Mr. Deane is still waiting for all of those customers to whom he extended credit to pay him, but then who is the other person?

I don't know who the "other person" is, but I think I met him last night. I went down to Williamsburg with a few members of my family tagging along. That particular night I was just photographing windows, and you usually cannot see much of anything on the review screen—I have to take the photos home and download them to my computer, and then boost the contrast to really be able to see most of the apparitions inside a house. My family could not see any results, and so they began to express doubts that ghosts were even real. So the very next house we came to was the Elkanah Deane House, and as I set up my camera, my sister and my niece got out their iPhones to take a photograph. But my sister could not see the house at all through the live review screen because something was blocking the view. She kept saying that she couldn't understand why she couldn't see the house, because she was pointing the iPhone right at it. Then she realized why: she saw a face on the screen of her iPhone. Whenever she would move the iPhone to view the house, the face would move with her—just a fraction of a second behind. There was an apparition standing right in front of her—or inside the camera's sensors, and the iPhone was picking up all the details of its face as if it were a live person. My niece cried out, "Mom, you can't see the house because there is a ghost standing right in front of you!" She moved her arms through the area right in front of the phone, but none of us could see anything at that moment. She immediately called us all over to see what her camera was picking up, and every one of us could see the face of an African-American male standing right in front of her camera. I urged her to quickly take some photos, and she

tried to, but she did not have the camera set right—and she got nothing. I went over to my camera to see if I could photograph the apparition, when evidently the ghost got too close to my wife. She felt a cold chill that started at her neck and went down her spine, and that's when she demanded that we quickly move on. They all scattered very quickly because we all began to feel the cold—not just any cold but an icy cold as if something was sucking the heat right out of our bodies—with the fear of the unknown quickly overriding the curiosity to see the ghost. I had to abandon my attempt and move on. This was one of the most incredible moments I've ever had as a ghost photographer, and yet I have nothing to show for it! So the next time you have doubts about the existence of the paranormal, you might want to keep them to yourself . . . or you may get a personal demonstration of what the supernatural really is—have you ever felt the touch of a ghost? How would you like an icy chill to roll right down your spine?

Figure 6: Here's a photograph of the Elkanah Deane House, with a bright blue orb inside the central upstairs window. It's strange how the orb is faded inside the central pane and bright on both the left and right windowpanes; perhaps it's the angle of the photo or the distortion of the original glass used in the windows. Notice also the apparition on the rooftop by the left chimney; this is the first home that I've captured two apparitions in the same photograph—but it will not be the last. I wonder if the person in the living room (bottom left) knows about the apparition inside the upstairs window or the one on the roof?

Figure 6a: Here is the same photo cropped to show an otherworldly glow—the blue orb inside the window. I thought it strange that the pane at the bottom center is dark with panes on the right and left glowing blue; is it the distortion of the eighteenth-century glass, or something else? Or perhaps it has a partial face with two eyespots?

Figure 6b: Here is the photo of the Deane house cropped to show the apparition on the roof by the left chimney; this apparition was very faint, and unlike the Bruton Parish Church apparition or the St. George Tucker apparition, this one needed a lot more boost in contrast to stand out.

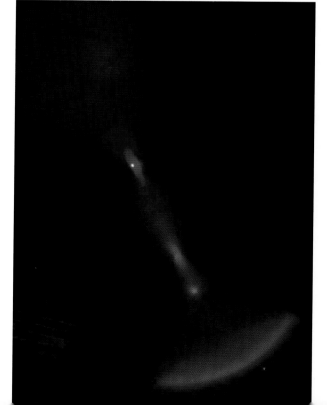

Figure 6c: The Dean House has something besides a fountain-shaped apparition on the roof and a bright blue orb in the central upstairs window; on the first floor left front window there are some faces in the pane—some rather unpleasant, if not ominous ones; one looks like an angry women, another a partial face of a man, and a partial face that looks more like a skull than a face.

Figure 6d: Something you will see more than once in this book is the appearance of multiple faces and eyes in one window—it seems like they are competing to appear over top of each other. Oftentimes, you will only see partial faces, like in this crop of a windowpane in the Dean House.

CHAPTER SEVEN

Whetherburn Tavern

The Man Who Married and Killed for Money?

History

Little to no background is known about Henry Whetherburn, but when he shows up in the record books, it's to apply for a strategic marriage license: he would marry the widow of the keeper of the Raleigh Tavern. Immediately he became the executor of the Bowman estate; in the eighteenth century all financial affairs were handed over to the husband when a woman was married—or remarried. Henry soon found himself the new operator of the Raleigh Tavern (1731), and the business began to thrive. He would later build and open his own tavern across and down the street from the Raleigh and name it after himself. Something must have happened to arouse the suspicion and mistrust of his wife, Mary, and she began to stow away cash to fall back upon in case something happened to the marriage. Henry discovered the "hoard of cash," as the *Virginia Gazette* reported, and in less than two weeks Mary Whetherburn was dead of a "mysterious illness." It was a major scandal in Williamsburg, and although many suspected that Henry Whetherburn was guilty of foul play, nothing was ever proven. Within weeks Henry found a new woman to marry—a widow of the operator of Shield's Tavern. Whetherburn now had another estate for which he would serve as executor. His new wife, Anne, had several children who all moved in with the new stepfather, but the oldest child would hold out for a while—till she became pregnant. She moved back in with her mother and stepfather,

and after having a son, she named the boy Henry . . . and the elder Henry developed an affection for the boy that would be demonstrated by what he left the boy in his will. More scandal? What do you think?

Now that you have a little inside information on the character of Henry Whetherburn, let's back up in time to when he was still married to Mary Bowcraft—the first unfortunate wife. Whetherburn bought two lots across the street from the Raleigh Tavern in 1738 and built a house on the two lots. Four years later, the Raleigh Tavern was purchased (remember that Whetherburn did not own it, he only ran the business in the building), and Whetherburn decided to move his business to his own building across the street. This is the building where Whetherburn discovered his wife, Mary, hoarding cash, and this is where she lived when she mysteriously disappeared. Probable cause for a haunting? Read on . . .

A Ghost Story

Colonial Williamsburg employees and tourists have seen an unidentified woman going through the upstairs of the tavern. In fact, one employee—the only costumed interpreter in the Whetherburn Tavern at the time—conducted a tour through the upstairs and walked the group downstairs. When he was finished, he realized that a couple had not left the last room upstairs and went back upstairs to find them. As he ascended the stairway and walked down the hallway, the couple came out of the room towards him.

"We were trying to ask a few questions to the other woman in costume in the room, but she seemed so busy looking for something that she would not answer us. So we gave up and left the room," the husband offered as an explanation for why they did not stay with their group.

The interpreter responded, "I am the only costumed interpreter in this building today."

"No, you can't be. The woman was there in costume; very busy and very distracted, but she was there!" the husband replied, and his wife echoed his statement. "Look, she's right down the hallway in the last room," he insisted.

The husband, the wife, and the interpreter went down the hallway to the room, and found it empty. The couple, bewildered, responded, "She must have gone down a back stairway! She was just here!"

"There is no back stairway," the interpreter responded. "You came up the only stairway in the house!"

The interpreter, realizing that some of the stories that he'd heard about the tavern must be true, offered this explanation about the situation: "I think you must have met Mary Whetherburn, and I believe she was looking for her hoard of cash that her husband found and took. She died mysteriously not much more than a week or ten days later, causing a scandal that even the local newspaper, the *Virginia Gazette*, wrote about. Of course everyone in the town thought that the husband was guilty of her death. She frequents the upstairs of this building, looking for but never finding her stash. I hope that I never find out what it's like to be locked into a task for all of eternity that you cannot complete. Many people have seen Mary's lantern passing by the dormer windows long after the tavern has been closed, as if that's just how she spends her eternity."

The interpreter said that speaking about ghosts and hauntings to tourists, at least when he worked there, was grounds for dismissal, so most employees refuse to acknowledge what many know to be true: Colonial Williamsburg is one of the most haunted cities in America. It has eighty-eight buildings that were built in the early to middle eighteenth century, more than any other city in the United States, and that is a recipe for haunting. Thomas Jefferson unknowingly set this up by moving the capital of Virginia to Richmond—in effect putting the Colonial Capital to sleep. The once bustling capital became more of a small agricultural community and a small college town, and people were in no hurry to raze the structures and replace them with larger, more modern ones. Moving the capital to Richmond preserved the colonial atmosphere of much of the original city, and enabled W. A. R. Goodwin and John D. Rockefeller to create one of the largest living museums in the country: Colonial Williamsburg. But wait—it's not just a museum for the living— you've gotten far enough into this book to know that! This is a place for the dead to continue living (how is that for an oxymoron?) as they hang on to what was as important to them in death as it was when they were alive. Would you like to hang around the place where you live now for several hundred years? Perhaps all of eternity?

Figure 7: Here is the Whetherburn Tavern on a night with a lot of low-hanging clouds; look in the upper right hand corner for the strange-looking apparition.

Figure 7a: Here is the cropped photo of the Whetherburn Tavern showing just the apparition. This one is unlike any that I've seen so far—a friend of mine thought that it resembled two hands, one cupped under the other—can you see the four fingers and the thumb? This was one of those nights when the low-hanging clouds had a reddish-orange color from reflecting the lights in the city.

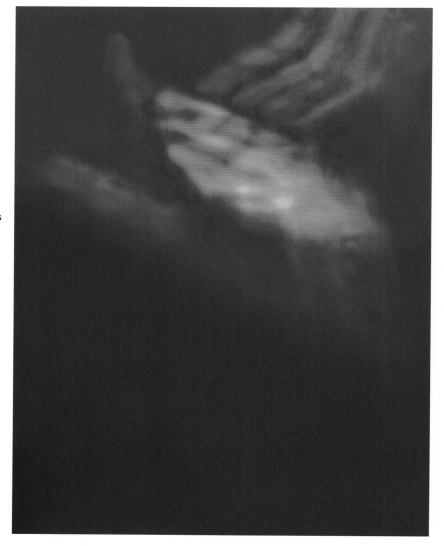

Figure 7b: Mrs. Whetherburn can sometimes be seen going through the upstairs hallway at night. Well, the tavern closes for tourists at 5:00 p.m. At the time this photo was taken it was about midnight, and there are no lights on in the building—but you can plainly see two windows lit up in the upstairs hallway as if a light is turned on. Notice the two tiny yellow orbs to the right of the windows.

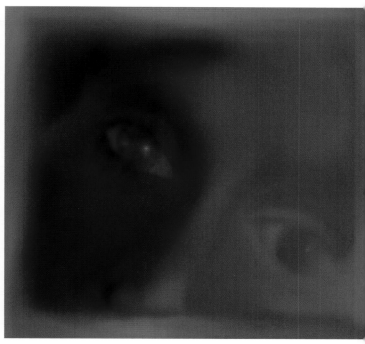

Figure 7c: In another photograph, a strange face shows up that crosses the line between human and ghost in the dark red color that matches the exterior of the Whetherburn Tavern. Perhaps this is Whetherburn himself—a self-portrait of a man of questionable character.

Figure 7d: All of the windows on the first floor are very dark, but with a lot of contrast the images in both this one and Figure 7e showed up in the windowpanes of the Whetherburn Tavern.

Figure 7e: Here's the second face in the first-floor window of the Whetherburn Tavern; it looks like a young face.

CHAPTER EIGHT

George Wythe House

Marriage Infidelity or Unrequited Love?

History

George Wythe was quite important to the formation of our country, and yet most people have never heard of him. One of the finest legal minds in colonial America, George Wythe taught the practice of law to both Thomas Jefferson and John Marshall (Supreme Court's Fourth Chief Justice, and possibly its most influential!) among others. He later became the first law professor in America for the college of William and Mary (1779). He taught classes at the vacant capitol building (before it burned down) after Virginia governor Thomas Jefferson moved the capital to Richmond. George was the unofficial leader of the Virginia movement towards independence. He was a delegate to the Continental Congress as well as Virginia's first signer of the Declaration of Independence. George Wythe played a key role in our country's march towards independence, as did his house: George's student and friend Thomas Jefferson stayed here as a delegate to the Virginia General Assembly in 1776. The home was the headquarters for George Washington right before Cornwallis's troops occupied Yorktown. Likewise it was the headquarters for General Rochambeau, the leader of the French forces, after Cornwallis surrendered at Yorktown, ending the Revolutionary War.

The last years of his life would be spent in Richmond; George served as a judge on Virginia's court of Chancery starting in 1791. A family member who wanted his inheritance sooner rather than later poisoned him to death; he thought he would help George to his grave a little early so he could start enjoying all of George's money—which he never got. A trusted slave woman discovered and informed Wythe of the poisoning plot, and Wythe was able to change his will and disinherit the man from his deathbed. Nevertheless, George Wythe passed away in Richmond and does not seem to occupy his Williamsburg house post-mortem. So if it's not George, then who is the ghost?

Ghosts and Other Insights

No, George Wythe probably does not haunt this house; according to author L. B. Taylor; it was a woman named Lady Anne Skipwith. She was a woman with fiery red hair and a fiery temper to match, and she seemed to think that her husband was fooling around on the side (perhaps with her sister?) while attending a ball at the Governor's Palace. She stormed back to the Wythe House where she was staying, breaking her shoe on the way. According to the legend, she ran up the steps and flung herself over the railing. You can read the tale of suspicion and possible infidelity in Taylor's book *The Ghosts of Williamsburg . . . and Nearby Environs.*[7]

A friend of mine was giving a ghost tour around Colonial Williamsburg one night, and among her company was a young boy of about seven or eight years old. After hearing the story of the suicide of Lady Anne Skipwith at the George Wythe House, he kind of muttered to the tour guide, "stepped on foot." The guide wasn't sure what the boy meant; she thought the boy meant that someone stepped on his foot. She asked him to clarify what he said, and the little boy replied that Lady Anne stepped on her foot as she ascended the steps. It was an accident; she did not fling herself down the steps! One little psychic boy clarified the real events of the legend of Lady Anne Skipwith—and he just changed the whole ending to the story! It's too bad the tour guide did not find out exactly what it was that happened at the Governor's Ball that set off Lady Anne and caused this mad dash across the Governor's Green to the George Wythe House. I asked the guide if her company changed their story to match what the little boy said; they haven't—I guess it makes for a better story to say that the woman flung herself over the bannister of the second floor in a fit of rage rather than to say that she tripped over her own feet. I have so many questions about other stories that make up the legends of Williamsburg that I would love to ask that little boy . . .

If the ghost is Lady Anne, she seems to hang out in the upstairs bedroom on the right-hand side of the house (if you are facing the house). A psychic friend of mine actually saw the apparition peaking through a crack in the shutters in the upstairs bedroom, but unfortunately neither my eyes nor my camera were able to pick up anything at the time. If you look at the photo on page 53, you'll see that I finally caught an orb there—after many tries I captured a large one over the house and a bright white orb over the face of a Colonial Williamsburg employee. (Some of the ghosts in Williamsburg are not as cooperative as others!)

Another author (Jackie Eileen Behrend, *The Haunting of Williamsburg, Yorktown, and Jamestown*) suggests that it's not Lady Anne Skipwith, but a woman who took care of French officer Colonel Oscar LeBlanc, who was wounded in the Battle of Yorktown. Kathern Anderson nursed the French colonel back to health and, in the process, fell in love with him. They planned to marry, but Oscar contracted malaria and, despite her best efforts, he died. So perhaps both Kathern and Oscar are the unhappy occupants of the Wythe House today.[8]

So it could be lost love, or infidelity that holds some spirits here. Perhaps all three characters are there—you never know—not to mention all of the people who have lived in this building since the eighteenth century. How many more stories of lost love or infidelity could we add to the list?

I would like to state another possibility: the Reverend W. A. R. Goodwin, the rector of the Bruton Parish Church and whose brainchild was the complete restoration of Colonial Williamsburg to create a living museum, had his office in the George Wythe House. Goodwin frequently talked about ghosts; newspaper columnist Ernie Pyle wrote this, when Goodwin "was alone, in the starlight, strolling in the night, talking with the ghosts, that he learned about Williamsburg." Goodwin himself wrote a letter stating, "You can train yourself to hear what they have to say." In 1935, Goodwin wrote, "I am in the Wythe House waiting for the hour to strike for the midnight Christmas-Eve service . . . One is not alone here. The Ghosts of the past are my gladsome companions in the near midnight silence."[9] Perhaps Goodwin is a part of the community of ghosts at the Wythe House now, trying to let the living know that there is an alternate reality, and that life extends beyond the grave—isn't that the message of preachers everywhere? Or perhaps he's communing with his ghost friends, counseling them on what they must do to leave the confines of this building to an alternate reality, wherever and whatever that may be. I mention this because in one of my photos I captured five apparitions at right about sunset—all grouped together. They were very difficult to see, even with enhancement, but it made me think that the five could include the two unhappy couples from both books as well as the Reverend Goodwin himself. He spoke with the ghosts when he was living; perhaps in death he's keeping company with the phantom friends he made while alive.

More Stories

I wanted to find something new from all of the stories available in ghost books and on the Internet for this book, and after a little searching, here it is: An interpreter who worked at the George Wythe House told me of his encounter with a ghost in the employee breakroom in the basement. Several employees were sitting around the table in the non-smoking part of the breakroom (before smoking was banned). Next to them, hanging on the wall, was a bulletin board for the employees of Colonial Williamsburg, where they hung papers informing employees about changes in work-related policy. As the employees sat talking, all of the papers hanging on the bulletin board moved from a vertical position to a horizontal position—quivering as if they were being blown by an undetected wind. One by one, as they looked at the phenomena, they began to ask each other with wide-eyed anticipation what would happen next, "Do you feel a breeze in here?" They all answered, "NO!" to each other's question, and what may have been thirty seconds to a minute of time seemed like an eternity to the frightened employees in that room. The very same employees were by the basement door when it began to vibrate up and down as if someone from the outside was trying to get in. When the same interpreter opened the door to see if another employee was trying to get in—or perhaps scare them— there was no one there. This could not have been a prank either, because the door was opened immediately, and a person would have to ascend an outside set of steps to escape being seen. The latch on the door rattled an additional two times, to which the door was opened just as quickly, with the same result. The ghost must have tired with toying with the living, for he or she left them alone after that.

Another story involved a caterer that was hired by Colonial Williamsburg for a special event held at the Wythe House. One of the specific requirements for that job was to have a lit candle in each window for the event. The caterer lit candles and carefully placed them in each of the windows before returning to the basement to make final preparations for the food she was serving. When she returned to the first floor with some food, she noticed that the candles had been taken out of each window and had been placed on the furniture nearby. She set the food down and once again placed all of the candles back into the windows as stipulated by the people who had hired her. Again she returned to the basement for further food preparation. One of the people who hired her came down to the basement. "Are you happy with everything so far; is everything as per your request?" she inquired as he walked up to her.

"Everything looks wonderful, but I did ask that a lit candle be placed in each window when we arrived . . . "

The frustrated caterer, went upstairs to set all of the candles back in the windows a third time, trying to explain to the man that hired her that she had done it twice before, but she wasn't sure that he believed her—he had that look in his eye. After all, there are no such things as ghosts in Colonial Williamsburg . . .

I can't tell you how many times I have come to the George Wythe House and gone away empty-handed! This home is very dark in the front, and I have found that sometimes I can capture an apparition on the side of the house facing the Bruton Parish Church, which is well lit. I do know that ghosts tend to gather around artificial light. The only time I have captured anything in the front of the house is when Colonial Williamsburg has special evening tours; the lanterns on the front steps are an indicator of that. I have captured some very interesting images on nights I have been there when the tours have awakened the slumbering ghosts. Perhaps you would like to take one—tourists have often seen the ghost of a woman in an eighteenth-century gown disappearing through a solid wall. Take a look at some of the mists, orbs, and apparitions that I have caught lingering around this old Georgian house.

Endnotes

7. L. B. Taylor Jr., *The Ghosts of Williamsburg . . . and Nearby Environs*, Williamsburg, VA: L.B. Taylor Jr., 1983.

8. Jackie Eileen Behrend. *The Haunting of Williamsburg, Yorktown, and Jamestown,* Winston-Salem NC: John F. Blair Publisher, 1999.

9. Ivor Noel Hume, *Doctor Goodwin's Ghosts*, Colonial Williamsburg Foundation. accessed November 17, 2014, www.history.org/foundation/journal/spring01/wythe_ghosts.cfm?showSite=mobile.

Figure 8: Here's a photo of the George Wythe House right after sunset. The lone, blurred figure at the doorstep is a Colonial Williamsburg employee waiting for special guests to arrive—note the lanterns on the steps. I wonder if she's aware of the grey orb above her and to her left (your right) . . . or the bright white orb that seems to be near or over her face . . . or the apparition that has appeared over the stairway inside? Near the large orb overhead are the flames of four very faint Spherical Torches.

Figure 8a: Here's Figure 8 cropped to show two things: the first is a Colonial Williamsburg interpreter who has opened the door and is crouching for some reason; and a white orb has appeared right over her face, appearing washed it out. The second is an apparition that appeared over the stairway while the door was open.

Figure 8b: Here's a closer crop so that you can see the apparition on the stairway while a Colonial Williamsburg employee has the front door open.

Figure 8c: This is a close-up of the front of the George Wythe House; notice the mist on the right hand side of the entranceway. The Colonial Williamsburg employee was waiting for a special evening tour, which is why the steps are lit with lanterns. She was watching me, but I wonder if she would still be sitting there if she saw the mist with a face just on the other side of the entranceway?

Figure 8d: Here is Figure 8 cropped of the "mist" on the right-hand side of the entranceway; some say that it has a face—what do you think?

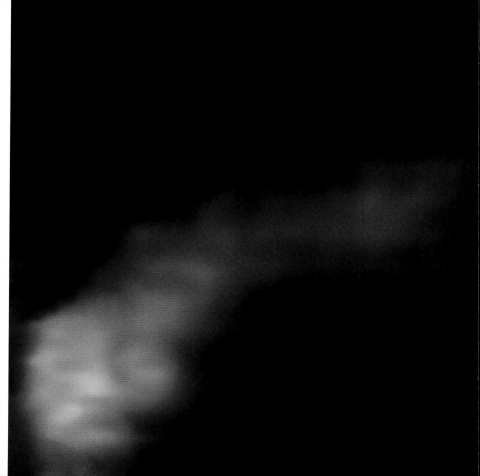

CHAPTER NINE

The Night Everything Changed

Paranormal Reality Has Changed Completely!

After working on this project for over a year (apparitions don't always show up for their photo-ops!), I was getting used to a general shape and appearance of certain apparitions. Any apparitions in the air around the jail, the Ludwell-Paradise House, or the Peyton Randolph House (not in the windows!) were usually grey-colored circles of various sizes and brightness—and some of the circles were misshapen. The apparitions that appeared over the Bruton Parish Church, the St. George Tucker House, and the John Blair House (among others) were shaped sort of like an old-fashioned fountain (or a fiber-optic light). On Sunday evening, April 27, 2014, I went out to my usual haunts (pun-intended) to try some new places and photograph the old places to possibly find something different.

I stopped at the John Blair House first, being the first house I ventured upon from the nearby parking lot. So far I had photographed a fountain-shaped apparition there that had changed very little each time I was there, so I was hoping for perhaps different colors or size to compare to my other photographs. To my surprise, the apparition had changed drastically in both color and shape. What I came to realize is that for some reason, on that night, all of the apparitions that were normally fountain-shaped were now circular. Because these creatures appear to be made of light-emitting energy, I would hypothesize that the fountain shape was meant to conserve energy, and by April 27, the weather had warmed up enough that they could adjust their appearance to the warmer days and nights. I am anxious to keep track of these same apparitions in the fall to see at what point they revert from a spherical shape back to a fountain shape.

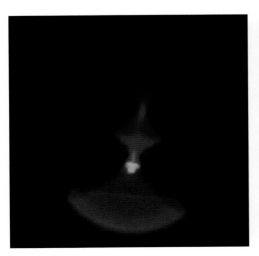

Figure 9: Here is the normal fountain-shaped apparition.

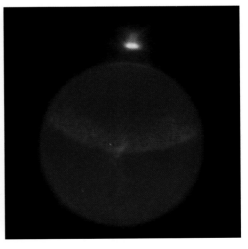

Figure 9s: Here is the circular shape the fountain-shaped apparition changed to.

I don't know what was going on in the spirit world that night, but Williamsburg was humming with paranormal activity. In addition to the change in appearance of all the fountain-shaped apparitions to a sphere shape, this apparition (see photos below) seemed to accompany every one of the circular apparitions: the circular apparition would be hovering over the roof of the house, and this red-colored balloon-shape would be on the roof or side of the house (the one on the left was on the roof of the John Blair House; the one on the right on the roof of the Geddy House)

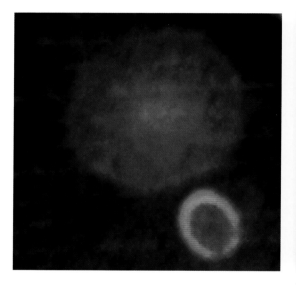
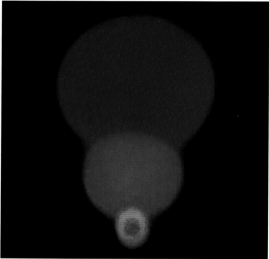

Figure 9b: Geddy House Red Balloon.

Figure 9c: Here is the John Crump House; large trees blocked the view of the roof, but the telltale sign of a Red Balloon-like apparition on the lower part of the roof indicates that a large circular or spherical apparition is hovering over the house. Look on the roof just above the front door and to the right.

Figure 9d:
Sometimes these Red
Balloon-like orbs are
hard to pick out, as
this one is on the
Roscow-Cole House.
The red brick make
it difficult to see, but
as always, the
apparition becomes
clearer when the
contrast is turned up
a bit. Remember as
you go through this
book to look for the
Red Balloon-like
counterpart to the
large spherical
apparitions!

Figure 9e: In addition to the appearance of the
spherical apparitions on the rooftops with the Red
Balloon-like orb somewhere on the house below,
some of the grey, circular and sometimes misshapen
orbs around the Ludwell-Paradise House and the
Custis Tenement changed to something totally
different; morphing from what you see to the
gigantic (in comparison) red apparition in Figure 9f.

The Red Super Cell

The word that I chose to name the large, red, oval-shaped apparition has a dual purpose behind it. In that double entendre, the first and most obvious meaning is appearance-based: it reminded me of a super-sized red blood cell. The second reason goes a little deeper, and it seems to me to be more than just a mere coincidence. The connection goes back to the idea that we have an electromagnetic conscious. Have you ever thought about why our blood is red? It's because within our red blood cells, we use molecules of iron to carry life-giving oxygen throughout our bodies. I don't think it's an accident that we have a fluid coursing through our bodies that is inherently magnetic, and therefore capable of conducting an electromagnetic conscious. As a Christian, I know the Judeo/Christian stance on this subject: the blood is the *seat of a person's soul, or their*

life force (Leviticus 17:11), which is why it was forbidden to consume blood. One thing I always wondered is why creatures like the vampire bat and the mosquito were specifically made to consume blood, but humans are forbidden.

Blood has likewise been important in ritual sacrifice of many pagan religions, but I have no idea if the participants thought that the blood was the actual seat of the soul. Some cultures have felt empowered by drinking their enemies' blood, but whether or not they thought they absorbed the souls of their victims I know not. These ideas and ritual practices were in place long before humans understood what an electromagnetic field even was, or the fact that iron was one of the best conductors of a magnetic field. I would be curious how other religions that believe in the immortality of the human soul, or as we address it here, the *electromagnetic conscious*, view what the soul is and where it is located in the body. What I *do* know is that after capturing small, grey, misshapen orbs at certain houses I was absolutely thrilled to capture these gigantic (in comparison to the grey orbs) red apparitions that had the appearance of textured light, with a bright V-shaped mark in the front third. My initial observation estimated that this apparition was around seven feet (or two meters) across, but just like humans, there can be variations from the mean size. Is it just coincidence that the Red Super Cell is the color of blood, or is there some logical, scientific reason for that, too?

The Custis Tenement is where I could plainly see the new and unusual shapes of apparitions that I had never seen before—not with the naked eye but on the photo review screen on my camera. The ones on the John Blair House were very hard to pick out on the review screen, but not so here. If anyone had told me that apparitions/ghosts/phantoms/wraiths (whatever you would like to call them) would look like these shapes, I would not have believed it.

One other thing changed that night: I began to see orbs of all kinds everywhere, including the Governor's Palace for the first time. If you recall, I said that I'd never seen any apparitions over or even near any of the rebuilt structures—only the original eighteenth-century buildings. But I did find out that the grounds of the Governor's Palace do have an original building—even though it is underground: the icehouse. It's behind the palace, with a maze made of English boxwood hedges right in front of it. You used to be able to go underground to see it (it was quite deep), but Colonial Williamsburg decided to lock it up from the public. On the next page, you will see a night scene of the Governor's Palace, with some orbs of the large and small variety to both the right and the left of the main building. On the left side of the palace (where you see a "Red Super Cell" in the treetop) there is a mass gravesite on the terraced hill where they now have a vegetable garden. During the Revolutionary War, when the palace became a hospital for the wounded American soldiers, 154 men and two women were buried in an unmarked mass grave, to be

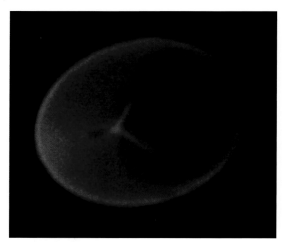

Figure 9f: I found a new shaped apparition at both the Custis Tenement and at the Ludwell-Paradise House that shocked me with both its size and color. It was a deep red, elongated oval that was the largest apparitions I had found to that point in time. I saw two near a small tree planted by the street at the Custis Tenement (see Figure 9g), and one up near the chimney of the Ludwell-Paradise House—in place of the small grey orbs that I had photographed there so many times before. I refer to these apparitions as the "Red Super Cell" because it reminded me of a super-sized red blood cell.

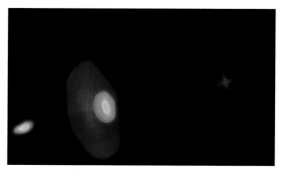

Figure 9g: This is a cropped photo of the apparitions on the roof of the Custis Tenement. The one on the left looks like an umbrella, and thus it gets its name. The one on the right reminds me of a sand dollar—two shapes I never expected to attribute to ghosts or apparitions—and they almost look like animation, or a painting!

discovered later by Colonial Williamsburg's archeologists. They also discovered musket balls with teeth marks—in lieu of anesthesia (which did not exist at the time), colonial surgeons would have you "bite the bullet" while they removed an arm or a leg shattered in battle.

Figure 9h: The Governor's Palace.

CHAPTER TEN

John Blair House

The Army of the Undead Marches On

History

The John Blair house, the first eighteenth-century home that many tourists see on the Duke of Gloucester Street if they begin their journey at Merchant Square, may have been the home of both John Blair Sr. as well as John Blair Jr. Historical records do indicate that it was definitely the home of the younger Blair, who had a distinguished career as a lawyer and a judge. It's interesting to note a custom of the day that lasted well into the twentieth century: unmarried sisters were expected to live with their married kin. This means that John's sister, Ann, would have lived in this home with her older brother, who was married and had a family at the time of the death of John Sr. Perhaps Ann continues to reside here long after her brother has gone?

Let's take a brief look at the younger Blair: he was a graduate of the College of William and Mary and went to London to continue his studies of law. When he returned, he became a lawyer and was elected to the Virginia House of Burgesses. Although he opposed the extreme resolutions of Patrick Henry in 1765 (against the Stamp Act), just a few years later he had gravitated to the side of those against the crown, and he met in the Raleigh Tavern with the likes of Washington and other Virginia delegates who opposed the actions of Parliament. In 1770, Blair again met with Virginia patriots in their pseudo-capital building, the Raleigh Tavern. He was the last of a long line of distinguished men who represented his alma mater, the College of William and Mary, in public councils for the State of Virginia. In 1777, he began his ascension as a judge through the Virginia court system, all the way up till George Washington appointed him to the federal court system—as one of the first group of justices appointed to the Supreme Court in 1789. Along the way, he was an integral part of the process that supported a stronger federal government and the passage and interpretation (as a Supreme Court justice) of the Constitution. Blair resigned the Supreme Court in 1795, and returned to Williamsburg, where he died in 1800 at the age of sixty-eight.

There are no known ghost stories for the Blair House (at least that anyone will tell), but as you will see from the photographs it is a hub of paranormal activity. I have seen a consistent presence over the house, usually in the shape of a colorful fountain or a Spherical Torch, as well as a few to sometimes hundreds of the grey orbs overhead.

Figure 10: Here is a photo of the John Blair House with the fountain-shaped apparition that loyally hangs out overhead. In the background, you cannot help but notice the army of the undead marching across the sky. Behind the ones that are really obvious are hundreds more that are very faint and can only be seen when you zoom in. To show you how random they are, and how quickly they move, in Figure 10a there was only the fountain-shaped apparition and one other orb. (These orbs usually appear as grey-colored, misshapen circles, but since it was not quite dark, they appear blue. This is because they are really transparent and take on the color around them. Remember the one at the jail in front of the brick chimney?) With mass gravesites from both the Revolutionary and Civil Wars close by, could this be an army (from one or both wars) of the undead marching across the Williamsburg skies?

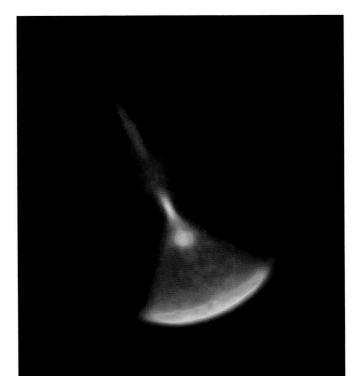

Figure 10a: Here is Figure 10 cropped to show a close-up of the John Blair House apparition.

Figure 10b: Here is a second photo of the John Blair House; the apparition has changed drastically! Notice that the sky has a large Spherical Torch apparition in place of the fountain-shaped one, as well as a few orbs (some are easy to see and others are very faint). Take a look on the roof of the house for two apparitions: notice both the Red Balloon apparition as well as the Yellow Umbrella; can you find them?

Figure 10c: Here is a close-up of the large spherical John Blair House apparition.

Figure 10d: I found this couple in an upstairs window of the John Blair House.

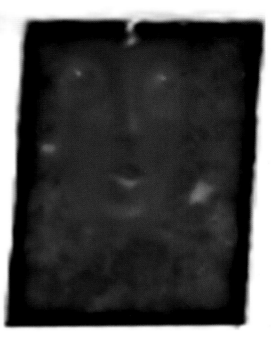

Figure 10e: In the same window, different pane, this wide-eyed apparition made his appearance known.

Figure 10f: This is the John Blair kitchen, a separate building from the house that sits to the side and back of the main house. In colonial America, people wealthy enough to do so built kitchens separate from their houses because they cooked with fire, and the added heat in the home during Virginia's hot, muggy summers would make the house unbearable to stay in. Notice the Red Super Cell to the right of the kitchen with the Yellow Umbrella (a little faded under the bright light of the full moon) sitting on the roof of the kitchen. Notice that the gable window on the right is open; look at Figure 10g to see what I captured inside.

Figure 10g: The central, elongated face reminds me of a reflection in a distorted mirror (or the computer app that distorts the appearance of your face). The face to the right has one eye (the left) that looks human and one eye (the right) that looks like an animal's eye. The apparitions on the left resemble snakeheads—what do you think?

CHAPTER ELEVEN

Custis Tenement

The Washington Connection & the Electric Eyes

History

Have you ever heard the name "Custis" before? Perhaps you have as part of another name: Martha Dandridge Custis—and a little later "Washington." Martha Dandridge married Daniel Parke Custis, one of the richest men in all of Virginia. The story goes that Daniel brought quite a few women home to his father, John Custis, for his approval to marry, and Colonel John Custis disapproved of them all. Now you're asking yourself, "Why does Daniel need his father's approval?" Because John held the purse strings, and he could very easily disinherit his son of all that money and property, including this rental home on the Duke of Gloucester Street, almost across from the Bruton Parish Church. But it seems that Martha could be quite persuasive, because she talked Daniel into allowing her to meet with his father, John, for tea one afternoon. After tea with Colonel John Custis, she persuaded him to allow her to marry Daniel. She and Daniel were married in 1750 when Martha was at the ripe old age of nineteen. She and Daniel had four children together before he died suddenly just seven years later; unfortunately, two of their children died quite young too, not unusual in the eighteenth century. Daniel (Sr.) and his two children, Daniel (Jr.), who died at the age of three, and Francis, who died at the age of four, are buried in a choice spot right next to the Bruton Parish Church, with a spot waiting for his wife Martha when she died.

Martha was only twenty-six when she became a widow—the wealthiest widow in all of Virginia. In the eighteenth century, when a widow married a man (remember Whetherburn?) she turned the purse strings over to him. So a young, pretty widow with lots of money and property was now available, and quite a few men came courting. But it seems that two years later Martha fell for a very tall, dashing colonel who was said to be the best dancer in all of Virginia: George Washington. They married in 1759, and George became a stepfather to the two remaining Custis children. (Martha and George never had any children together.) In just four short months after they married Martha moved to northern Virginia (Mount Vernon) with George. (By the way, she would leave her grave in Williamsburg next to first husband, Daniel, empty—she chose instead to be buried next to her second husband, George, in Mount Vernon. Daniel has been seen roaming the graveyard at the Bruton Parish Church, with a small child in each hand, looking intently at each grave, as if he were looking for someone—perhaps Martha? If you happen to see him going through the gravesites, perhaps you can be bold enough to tell him that Martha is in a grave up in northern Virginia with husband number two . . .)

The original Custis Tenement burned down in 1776, probably still under the ownership of both George and Martha—but by that time, George had a war to take care of. In fact, the fire was due to the carelessness of soldiers who were quartered there. Edmund Randolph wrote a letter to George Washington informing him of the fire, stating that the new country should be responsible for restitution for the damage incurred. The property passed from John Custis to his son, Daniel, to Daniel's widow, Martha, then it came under George Washington's care until it was evidently sold to a John Dixon—although there does not seem to be a record of the sale. The next house was built sometime after 1815. The word tenement means a rental place, and although it was in the possession of Martha Dandridge Custis Washington, there is no record of the Washingtons ever staying there.

Ghosts and Insights

Yes, some of the owners of this house (like the Custis family and the Washingtons) bear great interest to many people, but there are no ghost stories to go with this property—that we know of. Yet you will see the evidence of several apparitions that still seem to claim ownership of this property; whether these supernatural owners generate as much interest as the Washingtons, we will never know. Whatever the origin, you will observe a green ghost that has a very different shape from any of the apparitions that you have seen thus far . . . in an eighteenth century town you will find something that looks like it came from a science fiction movie about the future. In fact, when I first saw the object, I was wondering if it was perhaps a UFO. After seeing so many different shapes, colors, and sizes of apparitions, I am inclined to classify it as an unidentified hovering apparition (UHA). You will see some very different anomalies that may have taken residence here too, including one that resembles an umbrella and another—well, you will see . . .

Daniel Custis, as I mentioned before, has been seen strolling through the graveyard with a small child on each hand. If you recall, he and two of his children are buried on the north side of the Bruton Parish Church (although the inscription in the stone has faded, you can still see it when the church yard is open). The family plot was also to include his much younger wife, Martha, but she decided to share her eternal resting place with her second husband, George Washington. So the ghost of the former owner of this building has been seen hanging out in the graveyard that is almost across the street from this house, but the present supernatural occupants have not been identified. This is the first building where I encountered the "Red Super Cell" apparition, the "Yellow Umbrella," and the "Sand Dollar." It is also the first and only place where I have seen the apparition on the next page, which looks more like a green UFO than a ghostly apparition. I wonder how many times apparitions have been mistaken for UFOs in the past? As you will later see, sometimes the ghostly apparitions inside these haunted buildings also look quite a bit like the aliens that some people have seen and described. What do think? Is it an apparition or a UFO? Is the photo in the right book?

Finally, the two apparitions that I've captured inside the house have something in common: although they look very different, they both have glowing, electric eyes. One apparition is a recognizable face—except for the piercing eyes; I haven't seen eyes as intimidating as this since the Peyton Randolph House. The other apparition has the appearance of a classic white, except instead of the usual eyespots, the ghost has re-created eyes that look like small halogen lights; there's something otherworldly about the apparitions on the inside and the outside of this house—no matter who owned it! It's funny, but the first time that I saw the "Red Super Cell," I thought it was huge in comparison to what I had seen before. But as you will find out a little later on, you will see apparitions so huge they are the size of large buildings, and a wide-angle lens could only capture a quarter of them!

Figure 11: Here is a photograph of the Custis Tenement, with the green apparition in the upper right. Notice that it is not alone.

Figure 11a: Here is Figure 10h cropped to see the apparition, which reminds me of a flying saucer.

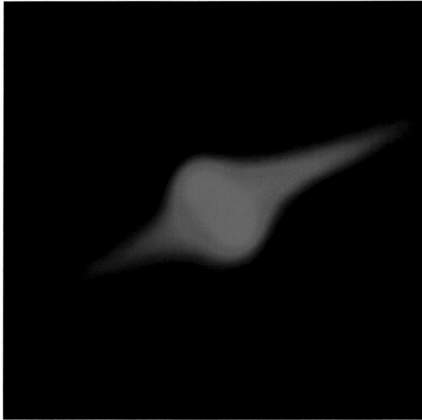

Figure 11b: Here is a photograph of the Custis Tenement; I moved just a little to the right to catch the whole Red Super Cell. Notice the Yellow Unbrella-like apparition as well as the gigantic (in comparison) Red Super Cell orb to the right by the tree. If you look closely, you can also see a red disk by the right chimney; and the green orb that resembled a flying saucer is nowhere to be seen.

Figure 11c: Here is a closer look at the Custis Tenement roof, which seems to be a gathering place for strange, otherworldly shapes. If you look behind the Red Super Cell orb, you can see another one of similar size and shape, although most of it is hidden behind the tree. Look also for the two red spheres on the left side of the tree.

Figure 11d: The Custis Tenement has no legends or ghost stories that might identify this apparition, but she is memorable with the fiercely glowing eyes.

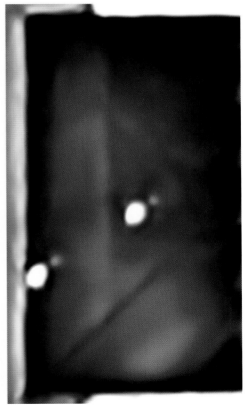

Figure 11e: In the same window, different pane, this wide-eyed apparition made his appearance known.

CHAPTER TWELVE

Ludwell-Paradise House

Madness and Money

History

The person of interest in this home, built in 1755, seems to be Lucy Ludwell, who later added the name Paradise after becoming the wife of John Paradise. Lucy's father, Phillip Ludwell III, was a very wealthy man who owned Greensprings Plantation and eight other farms in the area. He was a member of the Governor's Council, the House of Burgesses, and was one of the original trustees of the city of Williamsburg when it was formed in 1699. Lucy, born into wealth and privilege, was a very haughty woman, who because of her wealth, was bestowed with the adjective "eccentric"—rather than *crazy*. In the eighteenth and early nineteenth century, most people could count the number of times they bathed in one year on one hand. The belief was that if you washed away the oil from your pores, you would open your body up to disease. (Yes I know, they must have smelled great.) They also believed that getting water in your ears would turn your brain to mush, so bathing was not very frequent. But Lucy seemed to ignore the prevailing thought from her day, with an obsessive-compulsive need to bathe more times in one day than many of her peers did in one year! She spent most of her life in London with her husband, renting her Williamsburg home while they were away. For a while, starting in 1773, the publishers of the *Virginia Gazette* (still in existence today), both lived in and printed the newspaper from this house. Ten years after her husband died she returned to Virginia (1805). Because she and her husband

were squarely on the side of England regarding the independence of the American colonies, her home was confiscated by the State of Virginia. But the governor of Virginia allowed her to return to her home in 1805. She had her fancy carriage brought over from England when she returned to the United States and had it reassembled on her back porch. She would have guests come over to her home to have a "carriage ride"; her servants would move the carriage back and forth across the length of her back porch with Lucy and her guests inside. She would also borrow new hats and dresses from other women of means in Williamsburg when her own funds began to run low; she would return the borrowed items with small holes in them so that they could not be worn again. I cannot tell what the final deed was that prompted Williamsburg residents to add the moniker *Mad* to her name when referring to her, or garnered her the notoriety of her final accomplishment: she did become the first female resident of Williamsburg's "Public Hospital"—more correctly labeled the insane asylum. By this time she must have confirmed the prevailing belief that getting water in your ears (from too much bathing) turns your brains to mush—at least for the people of Williamsburg!

Although she died at the asylum, it seems that she has returned to her home to—you guessed it—bathe! Whenever current residents hear running water in the upstairs bathtub that they are not responsible for—they know that

Mad Lucy must feel the need to be clean. The first time they heard the running water, they ascended the stairway to discover that no water was running and that the bathtub was bone dry. Now they are used to the ruse of Mad Lucy and no longer go up to investigate; they peacefully coexist with a woman who seems to be as mad in death as she was in life . . .

Insights

For the longest time, every time I found anything paranormal in my photos of this house, it was always just one very weak, sometimes misshapen, orb that floats by the west end of the house, usually up by the chimney. Ironic that such a strong, haughty woman has left behind such a weak, misshapen presence—if that really is Lucy. Makes you wonder what wealth and privilege gets you in the afterlife? I had to really boost the contrast in this photograph so that you could see this orb, so look at the left side of the photograph near the top of the chimney—that seems to be Lucy's hangout. But as you will see, the small grey orb underwent a metamorphosis—see this page and the next. The third photo shows a much more elaborate series of geometric shapes and colors, and if that weren't enough, the house's occupants kindly provided me with their faces in the windows; could one of them be of the mad woman obsessed with bathing six to eight times a day and taking carriage rides on her back porch?

Figure 12: Here is the home of Mad Lucy Ludwell Paradise, with the orb getting a drastic boost in contrast (on the left side of the house, up by the chimney).

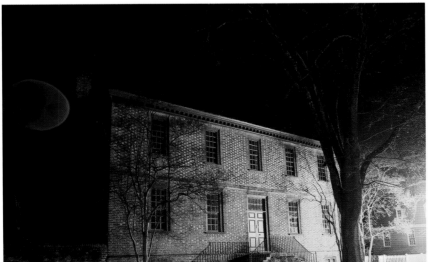

Figure 12a: Imagine my surprise to see the second photograph of the home of Mad Lucy Ludwell Paradise, with the orb getting no boost in contrast; I couldn't believe I was photographing the same house! Can you believe the size and color of the orb compared to the first photo?

Figure 12b: A photo that was taken after a large group of children passed, and it seems that Lucy wants to show off her best colors and shapes. Not only that, the next photo just may be a likeness of the now infamous eccentric.

Figure 12c: I obviously can't say for sure whether this is Mad Lucy Ludwell or not, but I would like to think that it is. If it's not, it's one of the many former tenants or owners of this original eighteenth-century house.

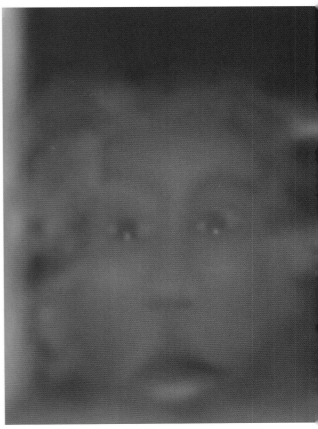

Figure 12d and 12e: In another window not far from where Mad Lucy possibly made her appearance, this gentleman made his presence known in over three windowpanes (most apparitions only appear in one). The face showed up and you can see that part of the lower face is actually coming through the window. The other two panes only showed a white, misty outline—you could not make out body features or what the man was wearing. I can't figure out why his mouth, as well as the woman's mouth in the top right photo, are hanging open, but this seems to happen frequently; stay tuned to see more gaping mouths . . .

CHAPTER THIRTEEN

Geddy House

Innocuous or Evil?

History

James Geddy Jr. was only thirteen years old when his father died, and he was soon apprenticed to become a silversmith (1744). Sixteen years later he bought the family home from his mother in order to start his own silversmith and jewelry business. He must have done well, because two years later (1762), he tore down the family home and rebuilt the present structure that you will see in the following photographs. Geddy became Williamsburg's most well known silversmith, and he catered to the wealthy class of Williamsburg and the surrounding area, including George Washington and the estate of Royal Governor Botetourt. He parlayed his success into other areas and became a wealthy landowner. As a member of the local governing body, the Common Council, he supported the Non-importation Agreement (our country's first use of economic sanctions—the American colonies refused to buy British goods as long as Parliament would tax them without political representation) and other actions that would soon lead to the Revolutionary War. James Geddy Jr. was an example of something that was uniquely American: he worked his way to the top, and was accepted into the gentry class because of that—and not because he was born into it.

Of Ghosts and Insights

A Civil War era woman—sometimes old, sometimes young and thin, "with stringy hair and glasses," according to a former CW interpreter—seems to show herself inside and out front of the Geddy House. She appears in windows and sometimes (although rarely) on the walkway in front of the house. Sometimes she will tap people on the shoulder (inside the house) just to let them know that someone is there. Perhaps she still waits for the return of her husband or lover from the bloody Civil War that our country fought, or perhaps a young teenage son who went off to war and never came back. I don't know if this apparition is the same woman, but look at the close-up of it and tell me if you think it looks like a snow-angel! I must have taken twenty-five or more pictures till the light apparition decided to make its appearance. My hope renewed, I began to take more photos, but to no avail. I think it was playing with me; this is the only photo of the elusive apparition that I captured after several different nights and quite a few attempts—until after April 27—then she seems to show up every night, not as the blue snow angel but as the sphere.

One evening, after the twenty-seventh, I took a series of photographs of the apparition over the roof. For the first photo it was its usual sphere shape, but in the second photo it became much more elaborate and colorful. I was curious as to whether the apparition knew that I was photographing it and was trying to show off, or if it was a defensive mechanism, as if to say, "This is my house; stay back!" What do you think, a defensive mechanism, or showing off?

Figure 13: Here is the Geddy House with the elusive blue apparition making a surprise appearance on the top of the roof. I took over twenty-five photos before and close to the same amount after, and this is the only photo the apparition appeared in.

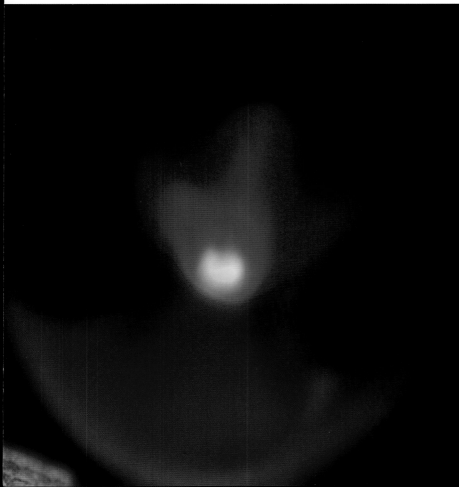

Figure 13a: Here is the same photograph cropped to show the apparition up close; it has a unique shape that none of the other apparitions seem to have—circular with three extensions coming from the top. It reminds me of a snow angel; perhaps it's the woman from the Civil War era seen in the windows of the home by tourists and interpreters alike.

73

Figure 13b: After April 27, the snow angel changed to a sphere like all the others. If you look down at the bottom of the page, you can see a few heads (I could not get all of the heads in the shot because most of them where middle-school children—it was more important to get the whole apparition!); there is a ghost tour right there. It's ironic that all of these people are listening and looking for ghosts—when the ghosts are watching them!

Figure 13c: Although retaining its round shape, it has gone through another change about one week later. This is the first time I have seen this elaborate of a round shape with new colors.

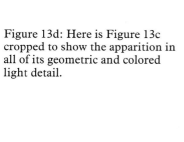

Figure 13d: Here is Figure 13c cropped to show the apparition in all of its geometric and colored light detail.

Figure 13e: This is something that I found in one of the windowpanes of the Geddy House. Although it needed a boost in contrast, a face with a rather sinister smile was apparent. Similar to the jail close-ups (except for the evil smile), they are smaller than a human face. I think this is a different entity from the one in the other photographs because the circular apparition was still visible on top of the roof when I captured this "face" in the window.

Figures 13f and 13g: I haven't seen the "thin woman" on the street or in the window, but I did see this strange-looking face looking out the front window. Notice the bright yellow orb at the nose; I just wonder if the face is being projected from that orb or not—perhaps like a hologram.

CHAPTER FOURTEEN

Prentis & Tarpley Stores

Phantom Store Clerks . . . to Wait on You

History

Archibald Blair bought this property in 1700 and evidently failed to erect a home or business within the twenty-four-month time he was allotted; he had to forfeit the property back to the city. He evidently either leased or repurchased the lot in 1718 or 1719 as an apothecary (eighteenth-century drug store). During this time, if you were a medical doctor, you were also a pharmacist. Doctors would often have their own apothecary from which they would prescribe and sell the right medicine for the disease or illness they were treating. Unlike today, doctors from this period would make house calls, and so they would have trained staff at the business to dispense the medicines. Back then you could get medicine(s) without a doctor's prescription: if you studied the medical arts or had prior knowledge of what medicine could heal you, you could walk into an apothecary without a script and pick up your own medicine—saving you the price of a doctor's visit. Like today's drug stores, these apothecaries would often sell additional items that were of the non-medical kind to increase profits. Dr. Blair went into partnership with Phillip Ludwell (Mad Lucy's father—remember her?) and operated an apothecary/store at this site till his death in 1735. By 1743, a partnership of William Prentis, John Blair, and Wilson Cary was operating a successful business on this site; father William eventually turned over the reins of the store to his son John, and John's brother Robert later took over store management duties until 1779, when they tried to sell the store (also called a storehouse in the eighteenth century). The deal fell through and

the Prentis family held on to the property until 1809, when it was sold to Robert Warburton, ending the saga of a Prentis-owned store in the heart of Williamsburg.

It's apparent from the photographs that one former owner, whether it's Archibald Blair, Wilson Cary, William, John, or Robert Prentis still feel they have ties to this long-standing store. This one-time gas station has now been restored to its colonial glory as a successful business under the name Prentis: I wonder if the presence you see over the store approves? I first discovered that apparitions will hide out in trees at the sites of the Prentis and Tarpley Stores. I finally found a way to draw them out far enough to make an appearance in these photographs.

Figure 14: Here is the Prentis Store, with the apparition hanging out in the tree overhead. This apparition usually hides out in the tree, but when it saw me, it came out in the open long enough for a photograph. It is a little different from most spherical apparitions, as you will see on the next page.

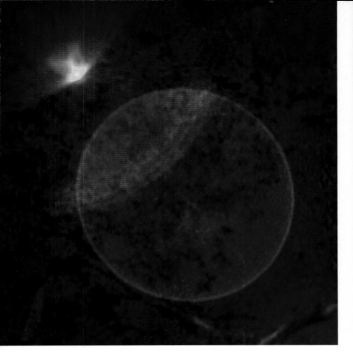

Figure 14a: Here is the cropped photo of the Prentis Store showing the apparition in the tree. It's transparent, and you can see the branches of the tree in the background. What's different and interesting about this apparition is that it has four distinct curved lines in the upper third of the sphere.

Figure 14b: In the front right display window I found this apparition, eyes almost closed as if sleeping. However, if you look closely, his eyes are open just a crack as if he is feigning sleep.

Tarpley Store

History

The Tarpley, Thompson & Company Store (henceforth referred to as the Tarpley Store) was built before 1755 (the exact date unknown), but the building has gone through a number of changes after Tarpley's death in 1767: in 1773, merchant James Hubard rented this property for his own business. In 1774, Robert Bruce ran a watch and clock makers shop, but later in this same year it was rented to Alexander Purdie, who—having just ended his partnership with John Dixon—started to publish his own *Virginia Gazette* here (at one time there were three newspapers—all with the name *Virginia Gazette*). Purdie also sold stationery and books from this store and, in 1776, put on a new hat: Ben Franklin, who made a special visit to Virginia's capital, appointed him postmaster of Williamsburg, so this store also became an official post office for what was then called the Constitutional Post.

This store and residence has served many purposes in its lifetime, and it seems that some of the former occupants are not ready to give it up—no matter what century it is.

Finding the Ghost

Knowing that this store is haunted, I had previously tried many times to capture something with my camera, without any success (likewise with the Nicolson Store). There are two large trees in the front that block the view of the top of the roof, so one night I decided to go around back and face north. I found a spherical apparition at the top of the roof there, partially hid in the trees, and after a few successful shots, it followed me around to the front. The apparition came midway down the roof by the center gable to check out what I was doing. I should have known why it was in the back of store though—that's where the chimney is, and they prefer to hang out by chimneys. Notice that between the front and the back photos the apparition got smaller—but the torch-like light also got much brighter.

There is a ghost story that goes with this store—it's an ongoing one and kind of a rite of initiation: whenever a new employee is hired by Colonial Williamsburg for the Tarpley Store, they are usually sent upstairs to do inventory first thing in the morning—because that's when and where a man usually appears dressed in eighteenth-century garments. Before the new employee is sent upstairs, he or she is assured that no one else is in or will be coming up the upstairs of the building—just to make sure that the new employee doesn't mistake the ghost for just another employee in eighteenth-century attire. After the employees in the store below

hear a shriek, or hear the employee running down the stairs, or look into a pale, shaken face that is asking for an explanation—then and only then do they let the newbie in on the joke: the store is haunted!

But don't ask when you go there, because they will not tell—that could be grounds for dismissal! Remember, there is a "Don't ask and don't tell" policy about ghosts with Colonial Williamsburg employees, because as we all know, there is no such thing as a ghost . . . But if you ever go to the Tarpley Store, please be aware that sitting somewhere on the rooftop, looking down on you and watching your every move, are apparitions that can be seen on this page and the next. Whether this one apparition is creating just one or all of the faces in the windows that you will see—I do not know. But there is one thing that I am certain of: You are being watched . . .

Figure 14c: Here is the back of the Tarpley Store showing the spherical apparition. I had taken photos of the front of the store many times and got nothing, so I tried the back—and look what I found partially hidden in the tree.

Figure 14d: After a session in the back of Tarpley's Store, for the first time I captured the apparition out front—I guess it followed me as I went around the store. It was quite close to me—it came down almost to the middle of the roof to see what I was doing, but it was smaller (and harder to see), although the "torch" was brighter. Perhaps it was the man who takes inventory in the upstairs of the store.

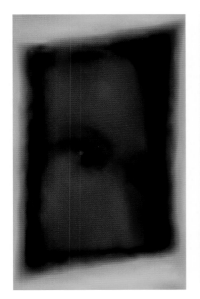

Figure 14e: Here is a face that appeared in one of the windowpanes; possibly a female looking at something to the right—the fellow in Figure 14f in the next windowpane.

Figure 14f: The previous apparition seemed to be looking at this apparition in the same window, just two panes over. I wonder how their lives are connected?

Figure 14g: I captured this apparition a couple of weeks later; is it the same apparition—or perhaps the same family? What do you think? The eyes were much clearer blue this time.

CHAPTER FIFTEEN

President's House

(COLLEGE OF WILLIAM & MARY)

Thundering Down the Stairs & Slamming Doors, or Seeping Out the Cracks?

History

This building was started in 1732 and completed in 1733, and is the oldest official residence for a college president in the United States. Every president of the college has lived there except for Robert Saunders, whose tenure only lasted two years (1846–1848); he seemed to prefer his home in Colonial Williamsburg, the Robert Carter House, which you will see later in this book. What's more impressive than almost all of the college presidents living there is all of the presidents of the United States who have stayed there! George Washington, Thomas Jefferson, James Madison, and John Tyler were welcomed there, as well as every twentieth-century presidents from Woodrow Wilson to Dwight D. Eisenhower; other dignitaries include Marquis de Lafayette (General Lafayette of the Revolutionary War) Queen Elizabeth II, Prince Philip, Winston Churchill, and Charles, the Prince of Wales.

Of interest may be some of the house's unwelcome guests: In 1781, British General Cornwallis sent college president James Madison (cousin of the future US president James Madison) packing; he made this house his headquarters for a few weeks before heading off to Yorktown, losing to the combined forces of France and America. Immediately after Cornwallis left, the house was used as a hospital for the French officers wounded at the Battle of Yorktown. It was during its tenure as a hospital that the house acquired another unwelcome guest: a French officer died in the house, and many believe that

he has never left the building. Just a few weeks into its use as a hospital, someone got careless with fire, as so often happened to structures then. Perhaps a candle left burning, or a lantern knocked over, or a spark from the fireplace, or even a chimney fire—the nemesis of wooden structures gutted the President's House in 1781. Since it was in use by the French army at the time of the fire, the French government accepted responsibility for it and provided the funds to rebuild the house in 1786. What many people don't realize about structures from the eighteenth century is that they did not make the exterior of a house one brick thick; brick walls were often several bricks (even several feet) thick. So when the interior burned on this structure, all of the brick masonry was left standing; all that would need rebuilt was the interior wooden parts of the structure and the roof.

Finally, speaking of masonry, a skeleton was found in the masonry of the house in the twentieth century by a maintenance worker. Although the skeleton was removed and given a proper burial, some seem to think that besides the restless spirit of the French officer, there might be another unwelcome guest in the house (read L.B. Taylor's book *The Ghosts of Williamsburg and Nearby Environs* for the whole story, including the testimony of several college presidents and their wives about the paranormal activity in the house).

Whenever I've photographed this house, it either has had every light in the house on (probably for some formal gathering of guests and donors) or it has had every light off with curtains and blinds covering the windows; neither extreme is good for capturing ghosts on camera. The structure has a plethora of ghosts around it, and I have captured a couple of white mists in the front of the house.

One of the ghost stories from the house's past includes heavy footsteps on the third floor from the ghost of the French officer. He is heard (heavy footsteps, like the sound of a large man in boots) walking and then descending the stairways, opening and then slamming the front doors—which are always locked when the phenomena occurs. However, when I photographed the front of the President's House, rather than a ghost opening and slamming the large, solid wood doors, I captured the ghost seeping out of the crack at the bottom. Has the ghost changed its modus operandi, or is this another phantom? I have seen this in the movies—ghosts seep through the cracks in doors, through keyholes, and through other incredibly small spaces—but to not believe it and then to see it in person was incredible. Notice too in cropped Figure 15b the bright orb about doorknob high has also left a

trail indicating it has passed through the miniscule crack between the door and its frame—yet another ghost? After the initial shock of seeing seeping wraiths, my attention was drawn to several faces that I captured in the windows: one of them may be the French officer from the Revolutionary War, or perhaps a past college president, or even the owner of the skeleton that was sealed into the building's masonry. Another face is a female from the home's past, and a third face looks as if it's not from this earth—an alien ghost? Take a look and determine for yourself; there *are* such things as ghosts, but *alien ghosts*? What do you think?

In the final photo I captured a ghost in the form of a human, but on closer inspection you can see multiple faces in this one form—a ghost *collective* if you will, an apparition made up of multiple ghosts to create the outline of a human—but why? Are they pooling their energy to create something much larger than they are capable of on their own? (This apparition was about six or more feet long—two meters.) That got me to thinking: Are the spherical apparitions that I see over houses and buildings just one ghost, or a collective?

Figure 15: Here is the President's House, all lit up for a formal gathering with a rather large spherical apparition that has a misty appearance—on an evening with no mist. This event has more than a few unrecognized guests—I wonder if the recognized guests know that they are being watched . . .

Figure 15a: I hope I didn't give you the impression that there are only one or two apparitions at the President's House. If you look at another angle, you can see a virtual plethora of apparitions overhead, and I didn't even have to turn up the contrast very much. I wonder if any of the guests heard strange noises on this particular night . . .

Figure 15c: This next ghost is hanging by the side window where all the action is—the president and all of his guests. Doesn't this apparition look more like a flying saucer?

Figure 15b: In the past one of the ghosts at the President's House of the College of William and Mary descends the stairways from the third floor and then opens and slams these heavy front doors. Now it seems to be seeping out the crack at the bottom; could it be a different ghost?

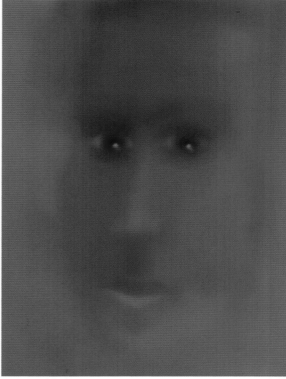

Figure 15d: Is this the face of the French officer, who perished on the third floor, or is it the face of a past president of William and Mary, or perhaps the owner of the skeleton trapped in the masonry?

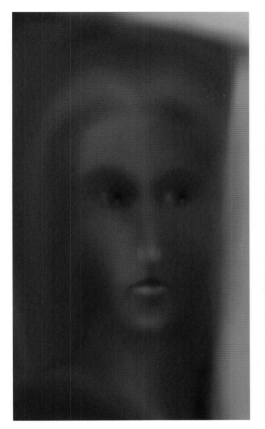

Figure 15e: Is this a former wife (or mistress) of one of the college's past presidents, or perhaps even a former student of the college (now officially a university).

Figure 15f: This rather small apparition has some very non-human characteristics; is it human . . . or alien? Is there such a thing as alien ghosts? What do you think?

Figure 15g: This ghost was in a tree to the right of the President's House; although it looks like the figure of one ghost, if you look closely, it looks like it is made up of more than a few ghosts—a ghost "collective" if you will. How many faces (formed or still forming) can you count that make up this one apparition?

CHAPTER SIXTEEN

Brafferton Building

(COLLEGE OF WILLIAM & MARY)

Where Have All the Indian Boys Gone?

History

The Brafferton building sits on the campus of the College of William and Mary, right across from the President's House. One of the requirements of William and Mary's charter (1693) was to educate Native American boys; included in the education was teaching them about Christianity. The hope was to make some of the boys into missionaries to their own people. Classes were taught in the beginning at temporary quarters, then later at the Wren building. Finally, in an endowment from Robert Boyle, a building was built specifically for that purpose in 1723. The executors of the estate of Boyle, a famous English scientist, purchased a Yorkshire manor called the Brafferton from the funds of Boyle's estate, and used the annual income from the manor to build and fund the Indian school—hence the name. The large room on the first floor was used as a classroom; the other two rooms were likely used as an apartment for the schoolmaster. The upstairs was used as a dormitory for the Native American boys. The adjustment to a new language, a new religion, a new culture, and a new and completely different way to learn was difficult for the boys—not to mention the heavy wool clothing that the English made the boys wear in the hot Virginia climate. The boys were used to going bare-chested with a piece of cloth draped around their groin; the wool clothing was just intolerable, and some of them began to run away. As a result, the unhappy boys were locked in their rooms all night. Today, some of the unhappy boys seem to remain in the building—at least according to those that have heard the unexplained sounds and noises—such as Native American tom toms and sounds of children crying.

Out of all of these unwilling participants a legacy came forth: one boy was able to fashion a rope long enough to climb down from the third story of the Brafferton building. The boy removed the heavy wool clothing he was forced to wear and ran bare-chested across the campus. Some say he did this on a nightly basis and would return to his room in the attic; others say that he was running away from his English oppressors and was going to return to his village. Many think that he succumbed to one of the European diseases brought over by the English (because Native Americans had no resistance to them), but whatever the cause, he died somewhere nearby. The boy's spirit can still be seen running from the Brafferton across the campus.

There is a field that has been dug out in the middle of the campus called the Sunken Gardens; it's just a grassy area where students congregate to socialize, read, or even throw a Frisbee. This area was not dug out in the eighteenth century, so when the phantom boy gets to the Sunken Gardens, those who see the running wraith say that he runs out into thin air over the field. (A student guide told this story to me when I first arrived at William and Mary to tour the campus.) That may also explain some of the paranormal activity that you see outside in the following photographs.

Figure 16: I took this photograph many times and came up with nothing; then I realized that according to legend the Native American boys could not stand to be in the building. I also realized that I can usually only capture the apparitions from one direction—so I tried north by northeast—success!

Figure 16a: There are two orbs on each side of the Brafferton.

Figure 16b: Here's a close-up of the two orbs on the right side of the photo in the trees. Do they remind you of anything—something to do with Native Americans?

Figure 16c: There are lots of apparitions inside the Brafferton; could these be the Native American boys?

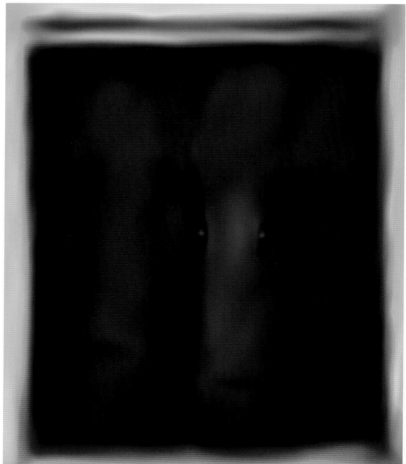

Figure 16d: During a second visit, I found a similar group of three with a slightly different appearance. Are they the same ghosts?

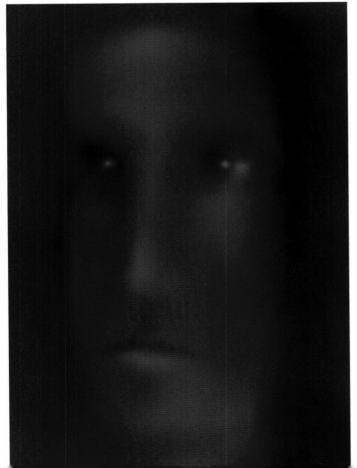

Figure 16e: Could this be one of the Native American boys—perhaps even the one that runs bare-chested across the campus and into thin air over the Sunken Gardens?

Figure 16f: At least two of the Native American boys did not like the confines of the Brafferton—I found them hanging out at what I now call the Brafferton Spirit Tree. Notice the two small Yellow Unbrellas with the two Red Super Cells at the top left of the tree.

Maybe the Native American boys are not the only ones to stay at the Brafferton—so who else does? Perhaps, from the looks of one of the windowpanes, some of their teachers have taken permanent residence at the former school for the Indian boys. The thing that immediately caught my eye about this photo was that it looks like an orb just exploded in front of the window.

Here's another Brafferton ghost—perhaps another teacher, or even the school's headmaster?

To me, this looks more like a young, wounded soldier; he could be from either the Revolutionary or the Civil War.

The top apparition appears to be from the twentieth century—judging from the hairstyle. I wonder how he gets along some of the building's older paranormal residents (like the fellow below), or for that matter, the building's living residents . . .

The Unseen Connections

What Formerly Seemed Like Two is Really One!

Another thing that changed after April 27, for whatever reason, was the appearance of several small apparitions that I had never seen before. I chose to wait until after the Brafferton Building chapter to explain them because of their unusual shapes: there is a larger one that resembles a bow, or possibly the side view of a Yellow Unbrella, and several smaller shapes that look like arrows or handles. Their shapes made me immediately think of Native Americans instead of the colonists, and that made me think of the Brafferton Building. Since April 27 and every

photo-op in Colonial Williamsburg after that date, these small orbs have consistently showed up in the photographs of many of the houses. To your right you will see the larger apparition that resembles a bow, and to the bottom right you will see one of several of the arrow-shaped orbs. I don't know if these small orbs are any of the Native American boys who lived and died at the Brafferton (recall that Native Americans were very susceptible to European diseases), but the bow and arrow shapes made me think of that connection. What do you think?

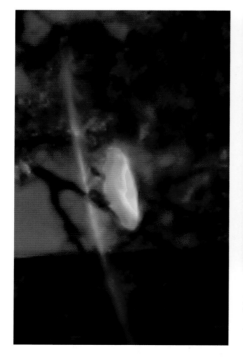

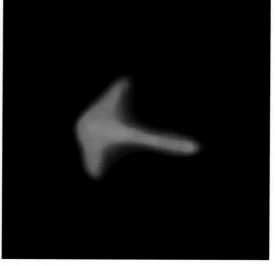

Figure 17 and 17a: To your right you will see the larger apparition that resembles a bow, and to the bottom right you will see one of several of the arrow-shaped orbs.

Ghostly Attachment—Red Super Cell & the Yellow Umbrella

Here are just four of the many places that these little apparitions have showed up. Just take a look at the next four examples. As you go through the rest of this book, look for these apparitions in each photo, and then see if you can find the Red Super Cell apparition—because somehow they are connected!

What I've come to discover is that just like the connection between the Spherical Torches and the Red Balloon, which is always one to two yards (or meters) below the sphere, there is a similar connection between the Red Super Cell apparitions and the Yellow Umbrellas. The difference is that the Yellow Umbrella part of

Figure 17b: At the Grissell Hay Lodging House.

Figure 17c: At the John Blair House.

Figure 17d: At the Peyton Randolph House.

Figure 17e: At the Prentis Store.

the apparition can be much farther away from the Red Super Cell than its counterpart Red Balloon. The Yellow Umbrella, if viewed from the side, looks more like a "bow," and the handle will sometimes look like an arrow—which made me think of the Native American connection. So everywhere that you see a Yellow Umbrella, somewhere, in a direct line from it, you will find a Red Super Cell apparition. Sometimes you will not see it because they are hanging out in trees, or it is out of the range of the camera. I have seen them over 100 feet away (thirty meters).

Figure 17f: Here is Colonial Williamsburg's Courthouse of 1770; notice that the Yellow Umbrella, which I believe to be the apparition's sensory center, rests on the roof of the courthouse and the Red Super Cell apparition is quite a distance away (distances vary for each apparition).

Figure 17g: This is an example of the same type of connection, but in miniature! Look at the size of the building on the previous page, and then look at the Red Super Cell in comparison to the one shown here. Compare also the Yellow Umbrella on each page for relative size. Notice that the size of the Red Super Cell on the previous page is larger than the cupola on the roof of the courthouse, and the one shown here is the size of about four small windowpanes on this very small, colonial house. The first question that arose—was this a child? Is the size in life directly proportionate to the size of the apparition? Or does it have to do with something else? What determines the size of these apparitions? (By the way, this is the Ewing House, and you will see a lot of strange faces in these windows a little later on in this book!)

Figure 17h: Here is a hotbed of orbs that include some of the shapes you have seen in this book—including the Bow, the Arrow, the Yellow Umbrella, and the Red Super Cell shapes outside of Williamsburg. The building is the New Kent Courthouse, but I believe that it was built on perhaps a Native American burial ground, a colonist burial ground, or perhaps the site where both parties fought and many were killed. I have never seen so many orbs in one place before—I counted over thirty. I also captured part of what must have been an enormous apparition—thirty or forty feet long! The Courthouse of 1770, an original eighteenth-century building in Colonial Williamsburg, on the other hand, has thus far shown only several apparitions, and it is over 130 years older than this courthouse. I suspect that it's not the age of the building so much as what happened on the grounds around it. Notice the three Red Super Cells overhead; if you would draw a straight line bisecting the "V" mark inside the oval, the line would travel straight through the center of the three Yellow Umbrellas down below.

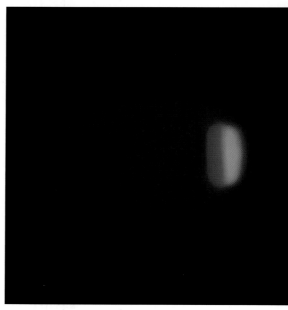

Figure 17i: If you haven't noticed by now, anytime I find a new apparition, I like to provide a close-up. Here's one cropped out of the photograph above. I have seen this apparition at the Bruton Parish Church, but not nearly as strong or well defined.

CHAPTER EIGHTEEN

Wren Building

(COLLEGE OF WILLIAM & MARY)

Wars, Fires & Crypts: Is Burying People Beneath the Floor a Good Idea?

History and Insights

The Wren Building's current claim to fame is that it is the oldest academic structure still in use in America. William and Mary is the second oldest college/university in the United States (Harvard is the first), and the Wren building is the signature building. It is also the first reported haunting in the United States: after the Revolutionary War, returning students reported paranormal noises and footsteps—attributed to the French soldiers from the Battle of Yorktown that died there. The mass gravesite of the French soldiers has not yet been found. Construction began in 1695 and was completed in 1700 and was the alma mater of several founding fathers, signers of the Declaration of Independence, and key figures in the newly found country, including Thomas Jefferson, James Monroe, John Marshall, and later in the nineteenth century, President John Tyler. George Washington also served as chancellor for the college—a position held by many distinguished Americans down through the years. As an alumni myself, I walked twice in cap and gown from the front entrance of the building to the back as part of an annual tradition for graduates (both for my bachelor's and master's degrees) and had a class in this building—all the while oblivious to the fact that the building has other occupants—the kind that you can't see. Interestingly, like the Bruton Parish Church, there are graves of distinguished Virginians underneath the Wren Building in a basement or "crypt" area. If you remember, Sir John Randolph, father of Peyton,

was buried here—as well as his son Peyton, and Governor Botetourt (from the British colonial period), whose statue is in front of the building. The Wren Building was a victim to fire three times: In 1705 (only five years after it was first occupied), in 1859, and later a deliberate burning by Union forces in 1862 to prevent Confederate snipers from hiding there. It was after the third fire that they found two bodies in the crypt of John Randolph—a mystery that was never solved and one of the largest apparitions I have ever photographed.

Besides education, the Wren Building has had other significant uses during its storied history: The Virginia General Assembly met here from 1700 till 1704 while the Capitol was constructed, and again for the period of 1747 till 1754 when—you guessed it—the Capitol burned down again. During the Battle of Yorktown, the building was a hospital for wounded French soldiers (If you recall, the President's House was the hospital for French officers—officers were often from the nobility class and would never share quarters with commoners—in this case the infantrymen). So we have a second possibility for paranormal activity, for we do not know how many soldiers died inside the Wren Building. In 1861, we have our third possibility: the Confederate troops were quartered inside, and it was later used as a Confederate hospital—until Williamsburg fell to the Union in 1862. The Union troops burnt the Wren and used its walled shell as part of their eastern line of defense. (Remember that brick homes built in the eighteenth century were built like fortresses, with the walls sometimes over one foot thick.)

Crawling through the Crypts

One tradition that is little known to the world outside the College of William and Mary is that a small group of seniors, before they graduate, will crawl through the tunnel that houses the crypts of important Virginians that I mentioned in the first paragraph of this chapter. Some say that you can get to the crypts through a tunnel system that houses the steam pipes used to heat all of the buildings on the Old Campus. Rumors, including an online blog post, state that forty or more years ago, fraternities required their pledges to use the tunnels to access the Wren Chapel Crypts and steal a bone from the interred skeletons. One student was said to have taken a whole skeleton, and kept it in his room. The college newspaper, the *Flat Hat*, published an article in the 1970s about accessing the crypts via the steam tunnels. According to the student reporter, the "slots" that housed the bodies were empty—devoid of any bones. Does that mean that down through the years fraternities have taken all of the remains of the famous Virginians housed there? I don't know, but what I do know is that there is a great deal of paranormal activity over the Wren Building. Students have left graffiti of their presence in the crypts: names have been hand-painted, and later spray-painted in and around the crypts to let future students know that they are not the only ones to take a dare and explore the dark, moldy passages beneath the Wren Chapel or to peer into the deep vaults. At present, a steel-reinforced door has been installed to prevent access from the steam tunnel; and of course access from the Wren Building itself is likewise under lock and key. But I'm sure some students will figure a way to circumvent the security measures put into place and gain access to the forbidden gravesites. Had I known about the annual crypt crawl when I was a student, I probably would have tried it. But I was unable to be a part of any fraternity because I had to work my way through college. I wonder how many of the students that have braved the vaults would have reconsidered if they could see all of the paranormal activity over the Wren Building that I have captured on the next pages? I have come to believe that the Wren Building, and not the Peyton Randolph House, is the most haunted building in Williamsburg. The reason why people remember the Peyton Randolph House is that there is a presence that is both powerful and evil; but if you examine all of the paranormal activity that I've captured over and around the Wren Building, I think you would have to agree that it holds the record for the most paranormal activity in one of the most haunted areas in the United States.

With the brief history of all the activity in and around it, you now have a lot of possibilities that would offer explanation for the paranormal activity at the Wren Building. But since apparitions can't speak; your guess is as good as mine as to the identity of the otherworldly occupants of the space inside and above the Wren Building, both the ones that look like real people and the ones that don't . . .

Figure 18: Here is the front of the Wren Building of the College of William and Mary. You can see the large spherical apparition in the trees over the large, central gable. It was nice enough to pose for one photo, then it disappeared.

Figure 18a: Since I've shown the spherical apparitions up close before, here's something different: a close-up of a streaking apparition inside the Wren Building window.

Figure 18b: Here is the southern side of the Wren Building; I didn't really expect much of anything here, but as you can see I caught the bottom of something really big; notice the Yellow Umbrella is a part of this very large apparition.

Figure 18c: Here is Figure 18b cropped, with the contrast turned up to see the light pattern from these orbs. I tried to aim the camera higher to capture the whole thing, but it too disappeared. This looks like something that is gigantic—if I can only capture the whole thing!

Figure 18d: Well, here is a wide-angle shot, and it only captures a part of two gigantic orbs that hang out over the wing of the Wren building that houses the crypts. I hope to one day capture the whole apparition!

Figure 18e: Something that I found in one of the windowpanes in the third-floor roof gables: he reminds me a little of Santa Claus. This gentleman looks like he is from the mid-nineteenth century when beards where popular for men in both blue and grey: Is he perhaps a Confederate or a Union officer or soldier who met his end here? There is someone in the next room over working—I wonder if they know that this guy is up there with them!

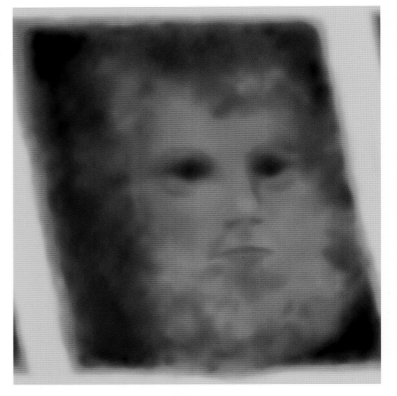

Figure 18f: I have only captured the face of the previous apparition in such good detail one time; usually it appears practically featureless.

Figure 18g: Here is the back of the Wren Building, all lit up for graduation. There are a few uninvited guests looking on overhead; can you see the odd shapes behind the central portion? Can you see the five torches? Sometimes they are very faint, and sometimes they shine brightly! Keep them in mind . . .

Figure 18h: I keep thinking, after thousands of photographs, that I've seen it all. Here is something new for me, something I call the Wren Five. Five apparitions, as if they are companions in death, line up over the Wren Building like five sentinels watching over the building. They could be French soldiers from the Revolutionary War, or possibly Confederate or even Union soldiers from the Civil War. Or is it five of the individuals buried in the crypt beneath the Wren Building's Chapel? I guess we will never know, but here they are lined up like five umbrellas over the Wren Building.

Figure 18i: Here is another first: The next photograph that I took, the Yellow Umbrella apparitions were gone and five much weaker spherical apparitions, hovering much higher up, were in their place. So my next obvious question is are these shapes interchangeable? Do the Red Super Cell apparitions turn into the Spherical Torches at will? I could not find the Red Balloon part on this photo, but these apparitions were very weak and required a big boost in contrast to be seen this well.

Figure 18l: Something else that I found that I never expected; I've seen faces in windows before, but never on masonry. There is what appears (at least to me) to be a face on one of the chimneys of the Wren Building, with a haunting look in his eyes.

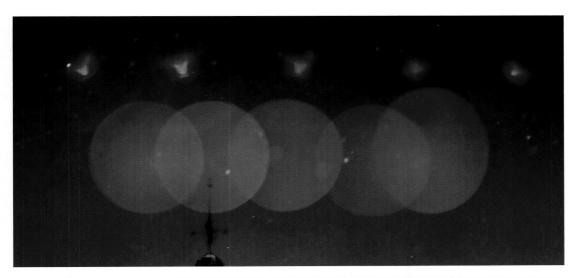

Figures: 18j and 18k: Here are the close-ups of the two photographs taken just seconds apart, the apparitions either changing their shape or moving very quickly. I'm beginning to wonder if they are connected in some way . . .

CHAPTER NINETEEN

Bowden-Armstead House & the Dominant Spirit

Can One Spirit Dominate Another?

Insights and History

When I first came to Virginia to work and to go to college I quickly learned that even now there are lingering feelings in the South about the Civil War. I was asked one time, "Do you know the difference between a Yankee and a damn Yankee?" When I replied that I did not, I was told this, "A Yankee may come to visit, but a damn Yankee comes to live here!" This little conversation, supposedly made in jest—but I still wonder— came to mind a few years later when I learned the history of the Bowden-Armstead House. When the Reverend W. A. R. Goodwin teamed up with John D. Rockefeller to start the Colonial Williamsburg Foundation, they began to secretly buy up property to accomplish their dream of a living museum of American history. Gradually word got out that property was being bought up in Williamsburg and that Rockefeller was behind it. The fear was that the knowledge of who was behind the purchases—one of the wealthiest men in the world—would drive up the prices. But there was one man who would not sell his home for any price, and that was Judge Armstead, the owner of the house we're about to see. He refused to sell his home because of where the financier was from: the North. When asked about whether he would allow the newly formed foundation to purchase his Williamsburg home, he replied in an irate voice replete with his typical Southern drawl, "I'm not selling my home to a dam *Yankee!*" Evidently the man convinced his descendants to be one of the few holdouts in the efforts to create Colonial Williamsburg, because

this splendid home remains the private property of Judge Armstead's grandchildren. The home looks like none of the other homes in Colonial Williamsburg, because it was completed in 1859. This nineteenth-century home has the large colonnades that were popular in the antebellum South prior to the Civil War. You will also notice that rather than a white picket fence surrounding the property, the fence is another nineteenth-century feature: wrought iron, painted black.

Today, large trees surround this house, so there is only one angle that I could shoot to be able to capture the house and the area above the roof. For the series of photographs that I took, what shocked me was that my second photograph, taken less than a minute after the first, had none of the orbs captured in the first photo. Instead, it had one of the large spherical apparitions coming in from the right (from where I don't know) and it took its place on the roof of this antebellum home. My third photograph has the sphere positioned over the house—and it just seemed apparent that this dominant spirit came and all of the other apparitions quickly vanished! It also made me wonder if it was Judge Armstead, firmly looking over his property from this vantage point to make sure that no *"damn Yankees"* would take his property from his family. Are these large, spherical apparitions the dominant force in the afterlife? Do the smaller apparitions immediately withdraw in the presence of them? Take a look at the photographs from this house and from the Custis tenement and judge for yourself . . .

Here is the Bowden-Armstead House, showing a sky with a trail of different orbs almost in a diagonal line from the rooftop of this Antebellum home. Notice the Red Super Cell and its Yellow Umbrella, as well as several other orbs in the mix. As these orbs departed, a larger Spherical Torch came from the right and positioned itself over the house.

This photograph of the house shows the whole home with the spherical apparition taking a dominant position overlooking the residence. Notice that all of the other apparitions—there just a few seconds before—have vanished. Are the large Spherical Torch apparitions the dominant spirits of the afterlife?

A different apparition makes its home at the front gate of the house, perhaps far enough out of the way of the house's dominant apparition.

Here is the photo of the dominant apparition cropped to show the details up close. Notice that this apparition is stronger than some of the other ones shown; it actually looks like it is made up of three spheres!

The Faceless Form

Now that you have seen the *dominant apparition*, which appears over the roof of the house and seemingly chased other apparitions away: Let's take a look at some more history and a possible explanation for the next apparition I discovered at this antebellum home—the faceless form. If you recall the Armstead family refused to sell their home to a "damn Yankee," referring to Rockefeller, and would be the lone holdouts till this day, because of bitter feelings over the Civil War. Knowing this, the irony of this story is the legacy and political ties left behind by the original builder and owner of this home, Lemuel Bowden, who was disparagingly referred to as the "Virginia Yankee," originally built the house. Bowden was a graduate of the College of William and Mary's law school, and became wealthy as a practicing lawyer in Williamsburg and the surrounding counties. He made enough money to begin building this house in 1858; with its classical features and wrought iron fence,

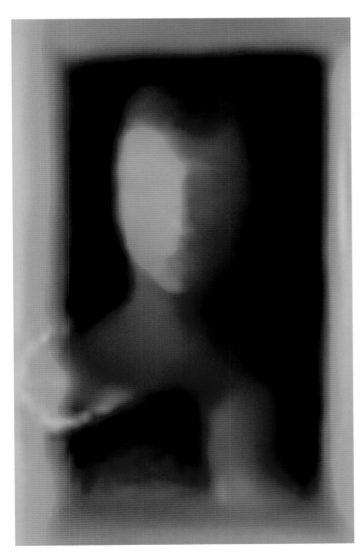

Now that one large tree in the Bowden Armstead house has dropped its leaves, it's a little easier to see the home. (The other tree is a magnolia, which does not lose its leaves in the fall.) You can see the front downstairs window from the street, where this odd-looking apparition made an appearance. It looks as if a face is trying to make an appearance, but was not entirely successful . . .

The first thing that caught mine was the enraged eyes: Is this an angry Armstead, perhaps the judge himself? I'm not sure if what's surrounding the head is actually hair, or if it's just the misty, ephemeral light that usually surrounds these apparitions.

The angry apparition on the previous page was staring directly into the next windowpane—at this female. Perhaps the afterlife is not as trouble free as we would like to think—at least for those that are hanging on to something in their previous lives . . .

the home's large size dwarfed most of Williamsburg's eighteenth-century homes. In the 1850s Bowden did two things that a Southern man just did not do: he spoke out against slavery and he joined the Republican Party. In 1861, when Southern states began to secede from the Union, Bowden had to flee to the Union-held city of Norfolk, otherwise he faced arrest as a traitor to the Confederacy. (His wife had died and he had already sent his children away to safety.) During the Battle of Williamsburg, the house was used briefly as a Confederate hospital. Bowden returned after the Union occupied Williamsburg, becoming the captured city's mayor, referred to affectionately by the townspeople as "Traitor" and "Turncoat." President Lincoln tried to reward Bowden by giving him a federal judgeship, which he turned down. But

in 1863, when all of the Unionist counties seceded from Virginia to form the state of West Virginia, Bowden was elected as one of its senators to represent the newly formed state in Washington, where Bowden promptly moved. It is possible that the faceless ghost may be Bowden's wife, a woman who remained in the background of all this controversy till she died. Who knows—they may still be struggling with Civil War issues in the afterlife, and perhaps that's the reason why they cannot move on. Although I can only imagine what's going on in the spirit world over this home, I do have photographic evidence that several paranormal occupants are trying to be seen. However, these apparitions shall remain anonymous, especially the one without a face, unless some portrait or family photograph that surfaces can put a name to the visage . . .

CHAPTER TWENTY

Robert Carter House

Horse with No Name

History

Robert Carter was an unusual rich man—he was more concerned about his principles than about maintaining his wealth. He was born into wealth and nobility, his formal education began at the College of William and Mary's grammar school, and he was sent to London to become a lawyer—and was unsuccessful, giving people fodder to comment on his lack of education and social grace. He moved into his Westmoreland County plantation home that he inherited from his father to become quite a successful tobacco planter after failing the "bar" in London. He ran unsuccessfully for a vacant seat on the House of Burgesses in 1752, but was appointed to the Governor's Council in 1758 by the King of England. That's when he found the need to have a home in Williamsburg, and bought one next to the Governor's Palace in 1761, moving his whole family there (and he had quite the family—thirteen daughters and four sons!). For the next fourteen years Carter worked on legislation, treasury accounts, and Indian affairs. The Revolution ended Carter's stint with the council, and he moved back to Westmoreland County to manage his plantation. Carter was a lifelong member of the Church of England—that is until 1777 when he converted to evangelical Christianity. He became a Baptist, and along with the growing trend of antislavery sentiments expressed by many Baptists in the 1780s, he voiced like sentiments until he did something unheard of in the circle of wealthy plantation owners: in 1791 Robert Carter emancipated all of his slaves. Colonial Williamsburg believes that it was the largest emancipation of slaves by an individual person before the Civil War. Robert Carter may not have been the lawyer his parents wanted him to be, and he may not have been up on either his social grace or his education, but he certainly was a forward-thinking man who was ahead of his time. Carter did not die here, but after freeing his slaves, he moved to Baltimore, Maryland, where he took up with another offshoot of evangelical Christianity and died there in 1804. But one thing is for sure—some former occupants of the house still claim the home as their own!

The only president of the College of William and Mary who chose not to live in the President's House on campus lived here just before the Civil War. The Saunders family, like all families in Williamsburg, dreaded the thought of a Union occupation. Any family that had the means to leave rather than live under the marshal law of the enemy did, including the Saunders. The usual thing for an occupying army was for its officers to select the nicest homes in the area to stay. The Robert Carter House was one of the Williamsburg homes chosen.

The Ghosts

The Union occupied the Peninsula, including Williamsburg, for the duration of the Civil War after the Battle of Fort Magruder in May of

1862. But from time to time, the Confederates, usually the cavalry, would raid and harass the Federals at night. During one such raid, the Union officer stationed at the Carter House heard soldiers in the backyard. He went out on the back porch and began shooting his pistol wherever he heard noises in the underbrush. The officer caught the sight of one young soldier's bayonet glistening in the moonlight and shot at it. The soldier, just a teenage boy, was mortally wounded; his ghost returns to the backyard of the Robert Carter House to reenact the final moments of his life in a repeating action that mimics the futility of war. Throughout the years since, the glistening bayonet and the dark, shadowy figure of a young Rebel soldier have been seen and heard out back of the Carter House. Although I did not see the gleaming bayonet, I did capture several apparitions hanging near lampposts in the backyard—could he be one of them?

A curious apparition resides over the Carter House; when I first came, it was on top of the roof near the right chimney. Then the spherical apparition moved down over the front edge of the roof to observe me. (By the way, the Robert Carter House is a dark reddish-brown color in the daylight.) Whether it's the same entity or a different one, another inquisitive spectre was observing me on the side of the house from the top of a downstairs window: a blue horse, sans ears. Everything in this window was as black as night except for this deep blue apparition that appeared in the top pane (I lightened the image considerably!). Since a horse would have no reason to be anchored to the house—if animals even have ghosts—why would a former human re-create an apparition of a horse? This horse-like wraith is similar to the bizarre faces at the St. George Tucker House (Chapter 2)— which is not to far from the Carter House I might add. In both cases, the apparition appeared to be on the outside of the window of the house; could they be wandering phantoms?

A photograph of the kitchen (a separate building in eighteenth-century Southern homes) of this antebellum mansion was likewise a surprise: a group of classic white ghosts, complete with the pointed heads, were gathered together and looking out at me. Although there were more than the three shown, I cropped the photo to show the ones that had the clearest outlines. Like the Carter family, this household was wealthy . . . with wraiths and anomalies from a world we've only touched the surface of understanding.

Figure 20: Here is the Robert Carter House, showing the curious spherical apparition, smaller and less brilliant than the one at the Bowden-Armstead House. Notice the characteristic "Red Balloon" part of this apparition can plainly be seen on the gable of the porch roof.

Figure 20a: Could this apparition be the young Confederate soldier that was shot to death in the backyard of the Carter House by a Union officer right after the Battle of Williamsburg?

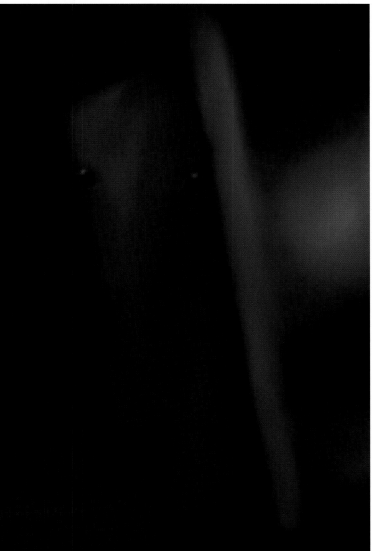

Figure 20b: This nameless apparition of a blue horse was looking down at me from the Robert Carter House; is it a former human—or do animals really have ghosts? (I lightened this photo considerably; the surrounding windows were pitch black . . .)

Figure 20c: These three classic white "Halloween" type ghosts looked on as I photographed the kitchen of the Robert Carter House—a separate building in the South. There were others inside, but these three showed up the clearest.

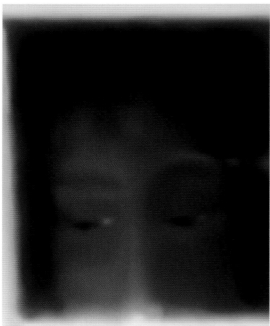

Figure 20d: Looking out the front of the Robert Carter House is this forlorn face; she usually does not show up this clear, but one night she decided to make it worth my while.

Figure 20e: Looking out the side of the Robert Carter House in the window next to the one with the blue horse, this apprehensive apparition looks to be from the Civil War era.

CHAPTER TWENTY-ONE

Taliaferro-Cole House

The Paranormal Gets Even More Bizarre

History

Charles Taliaferro was a coach and chair maker, but he seemed to have his hands in a little bit of everything: he ran a warehouse, a brewery, a boat- and flat-making business at College Landing, and a store. He also owned fifteen Williamsburg properties, and the home we are going to look at was built around 1760 and acquired by Taliaferro (strangely enough pronounced "toliver") in 1769. Taliaferro may have used this house as a commercial property, and after he died, his business associate, Jesse Cole, acquired the building from the estate sale in 1804, enlarged it, and boarded College of William and Mary students there. Cole, like Taliaferro, was a man who wore many hats: he ran an apothecary and a store, was Williamsburg's postmaster, and leader of the Williamsburg Freemasons.

Insights

Just when I thought I had seen everything, something new and even stranger came along to top what I'd already seen and photographed. The Taliaferro-Cole House seemed like a few of the others, with a medium-sized spherical apparition hovering over one of its chimneys and a few of the usual grey orbs floating here and there. Nothing unusual or spectacular—in fact, it was quite mundane and I wondered if I should even include it in this book. But the first thing I was stunned to see when I examined the photographs closely was what appeared at first to be a small yellow orb, similar to the ones I captured on the left side of the Brafferton Building on the campus of the College of William and Mary. But when I magnified the view to see the detail—I actually saw a face! I haven't a clue to whom the face belongs, but it was so strange to see a disembodied face in the tree on the side of the house!

In addition to the flying phantom face, I found something that was a little more creepy . . . have you ever had the feeling that you were being watched? This house was my last stop of the night—it was past one o'clock in the morning and I had already walked several miles around Colonial Williamsburg. I had that feeling, but I could not explain it until I got home and actually examined the photos. Two apparitions were at the house across the street from the Taliaferro-Cole House—and looking right at me! Although the photo is of this house, I am holding off all the details till the next chapter. But meanwhile, this house has a bizarre collection of apparitions, including a menacing red-haired, dark-eyed wraith, an apparition that resembles a gigantic piece of modern art (a geo-light apparition), and something even more bizarre.

After discovering a tiny face in the orb that just looked like a splotch of yellow light, I began to look more closely at this house. On the shutter of a downstairs window, to my shock and amazement, I discovered a motionless white dragonfly—with its wings out as if flying. Immediately upon observing the ghost dragonfly on the shutter of the Taliaferro-Cole House, questions began to flood my mind: Do animals have souls? I know, I kind of dismissed that idea in the last chapter with the blue horse; I'm still trying to adjust to this learning curve. Better yet, do insects, those miniscule members of the animal kingdom that operate on pure instinct, have souls? Or is this a former human soul trying to re-create itself as a favorite insect? Will I discover other apparitions that resemble animals?

Figure 21: Here is the Taliaferro-Cole House on a moonlit night; there is more to this photograph than meets the eye! Notice the spherical apparition on the left corner of the house looking down at me. On the left side of the house by the chimney you can see a glowing yellow orb. Imagine my shock when I cropped the photo to find that it had a face—look at Figures 21a and 21b! Across the street I found two apparitions watching me!

Figure 21a: A close-up of the yellow colored orb on the left side of the house by the chimney, just a little over halfway up. I'm not sure where the hair lets off and the leaves begin.

Figure 21b: This rather menacing, red-haired, dark-eyed person was the only face that I have found so far on the inside of the Taliaferro-Cole House.

Figure 21c: I decided to try the Taliaferro-Cole House from the back—and very glad I did! If you recall, the first time I captured a spherical apparition over this house, it was a much smaller size and rather plain in appearance in comparison to some of the others. This apparition looks like a piece of modern art!

Figure 21d: Here is the cropped version of Figure 21c so you can see the geometric designs and the colors.

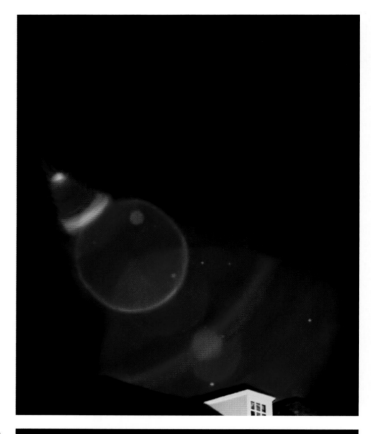

Figure 21e: The final anomaly that I've found here (at least as of this writing) is from a photograph that I took about midnight. If you have ever watched a dragonfly, you know that they are not active at night—and when they are active, they do not stay in one place at a time for very long. So what do you think this is by the shutter of the Taliaferro-Cole House, in mid-air, with its wings showing no movement? Is this a "ghost dragonfly"?

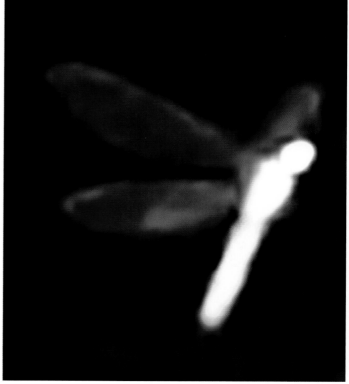

CHAPTER TWENTY-TWO

The Bryan House

Site of an Abduction, or Murder?

History

The first owner of a home on this site was William Bryan according to insurance records (in the eighteenth century it was called *assurance*), and a house was located on this lot in the early 1780s. There is not much information on Bryan or his widow, who lived in the home with their son Julian after William died in 1797. There is just a tad bit more information on the second owner, Jack Hudgins, who had a grocery store on this site. Anecdotal evidence about Hudgins (or Hutchings—spelling?) indicates he was a bit eccentric, including this statement: "He was known to be high tempered, irritable, and very crabbed." I have heard of crabby, but not "very crabbed"; but grouchy old Jack Hudgins was living in the home as late as 1861, with very little in the way of records after that. Could this home have been a victim of the fires set in Williamsburg by drunken Union soldiers, angry over the attack by a Confederate Cavalry unit commanded by Colonel William P. Shingler that took away their commanding officer as a prisoner of war? (The Wren building, as well as several homes and barns were burned. Other homes were taken down and the materials used to make officers' quarters for the winter at Fort Magruder.)

Insights

Do you remember the first photograph at the Taliaferro-Cole House, where I found something that was unnerving? I had that visceral feeling of a presence nearby, but had no idea who or what it was until I magnified the photos. Two apparitions were at the corner of the Bryan House, across the street from the Taliaferro-Cole House, right on the edge of the photo—and looking right at me! One was a woman, with her hand on the side of the house. Behind her is the face of what seems to be an angry man, with his hand covering the woman's mouth, as if he is about to abduct her or hurt her. Some things in the photo are quite obvious, and others are up for interpretation. You can look at and judge for yourself what your interpretation of the photo is; I wonder if this woman is about to be taken away by the man behind her—was she a victim of his anger and rage? Is this one of those scenes that keeps repeating itself over and over—perhaps for hundreds of years—as these restless spirits re-create the series of events that maybe resulted in the death of one or both individuals? Did I capture the reenactment of a murder? See for yourself . . .

Figure 22: This house sits across the street from the Taliaferro-Cole House, and is where I captured two very real, and perhaps one very frightening apparition. This photo, taken several months later, shows a Red Super Cell near where the apparitions stood—looking around the left side corner of the Bryan house. Notice that the Yellow Umbrella is on the front roof of this rebuilt house, with another apparition out a bit farther from it. On Figure 22a you will find what was looking around the corner, below and to the right of the Red Super Cell!

Figure 22a: Have you ever felt like you were being watched? I had that same feeling when I was taking the photograph of the Taliaferro-Cole House; here's what I found looking around the side of the house across the street. (I realize that you can only see part of the face of the man standing behind this woman, but I think it's pretty obvious that not only is it a man, but that it's a very angry man. Some who have seen the photo believe that the man has his hand by or on the woman's mouth as if to keep her from crying for help—what do you think? I've also had people comment that they see other faces in the photo—I'll leave that up to you to look for and judge for yourself.)

Figure 22b: A closer look at the man behind the woman shown in Figure 22a.

CHAPTER TWENTY-THREE

Ludwell Tenement

Revolutionary War Soldiers Out Back?

History

Tenement had a different meaning in the eighteenth century than it does now: the present day meaning is a rental property but is associated with the idea of substandard housing for the poor in a large building or buildings in a large city. In the eighteenth century, very wealthy people like the Ludwells would have homes built for family and friends to stay; today we would call them guesthouses—although sometimes they were used as rentals. The original Ludwell Tenement may have been built circa 1715 for one of the richest and most prominent families in Virginia at the time. The home survived until the Civil War, with one resident noting that the house was "pulled down, perhaps, like other houses in Williamsburg, by Yankee troops." Several things are very unusual about this home for the time—the first being that the kitchen was in the basement rather than in a separate building. Keeping a cooking fire burning all day not only heightened the chances of an accidental fire, but also made the house unbearably hot in Virginia's sultry summers. The second anomaly is that the chimney is off-center to accommodate a fireplace for the basement kitchen, and the chimney pierces the roof rather than being on the outside of the house, with only the fireplaces being in the interior—contrary to building norms in Virginia.

Most tourists do not realize that a tunnel runs under Colonial Williamsburg for the Colonial Parkway, a scenic paved road with river views (and without any billboards!) that connects the three points of the historic triangle: Jamestown, Colonial Williamsburg, and Yorktown. The foundation for this house has pilings driven into the ground to cantilever it (overhang it) over the tunnel. Unfortunately, digging the tunnel destroyed all the archeological evidence around this home before its reconstruction. The only thing that survived the tunnel construction was a part of the north wall (which faced the woods behind the house) of the home's foundation. By the way, this tunnel has nothing to do with Colonial Williamsburg's network of tunnels underneath the retail shops and restaurants that are used to restock the shelves and freezers—which is why you never see any trailer trucks unloading in Colonial Williamsburg—it would destroy the eighteenth-century ambience.

Here's just a little information about the original family that owned this property: Philip Ludwell II was appointed to the Governor's Council. He acted as Rector of William and Mary College and, in 1710, was appointed deputy auditor-general for the colony by Governor Spotswood. His son, Philip Ludwell III, was the next owner of this house, but he spent a lot of time in England, and this property would serve as a rental income for his family. You may recall his daughter, Lucy Ludwell, whose antics would later earn her the moniker "Mad Lucy," and who became the first female to be placed in the asylum built in Williamsburg. After the death of her father, Lucy came in to possession of this home, but she continued to live in England with her husband John Paradise, because she was against the Revolution. None of these people actually lived in this house, and since most of Williamsburg's records were lost in a fire, we have no idea who the apparition is that resides near and sometimes over the house. Since I have captured this apparition in the back of the house, sometimes hanging out in the trees, I'm going to give you two possibilities for the phantom's presence around this home, and it has to do with a tunnel and the woods behind the house next door: The Tayloe House.

Although John Tayloe II could not bring himself to support the Revolution, the woods behind his house served as an encampment for American Revolutionary War soldiers. During the Battle of Yorktown, wounded American soldiers were brought back to the encampment to be treated, and some of them died there. Some tourists claim to have heard the noise from these soldiers late at night, talking, laughing and celebrating—but upon going toward the source of the sound in the back of the Ludwell Tenement and the Tayloe House, the sounds stop.

If not the Revolutionary War soldiers, another possibility was a recent discovery that the builders of the underground tunnel beneath the Ludwell Tenement inadvertently dug up: a Native American burial ground. The Williamsburg Tunnel was constructed in the 1940s, and the burial ground—sacred to Native Americans— was quietly moved to another, undisclosed location. I suppose you can move the bones, but the souls just might be left behind. If one, several, or all of these ghosts formed an attachment to the hallowed ground, that could be the explanation for the wraith over the Ludwell Tenement and/or the ghostly gathering between this house and the Tayloe House— maybe another ghost collective?

Camera-Shy Ghosts

I've been asked why I don't just aim the camera up at the roof to capture the apparition up close, rather than taking a photo of the whole house. The reason I don't is because as soon as I aim the camera up at the roof, the apparition disappears; *they know!* I first tried to capture this apparition like that, and the minute that I aimed the camera up, the apparition moved up—so that I only got part of the sphere. So I aimed the camera higher, the apparition went higher, this time only getting the bottom third of the sphere in the photo. I continued this experiment elsewhere, with the same results. So the only way I can capture these dominant spirits, like the one you see on the next page over the Ludwell Tenement, is to photograph the home and then crop the photo to show the apparitions up close. I usually see only one Spherical Torch over small homes, hence the moniker dominant spirit. However, I have seen multiple faces in the windows of these same houses, so is it possible that the apparition is a ghost collective? I mentioned this before at the Wren Building, and I bring it up here because both stories attached to the house are about groups of people (Native American burial ground and Revolutionary War encampment) and not an individual.

A few months later I returned to this house to see if I could capture something besides the spherical apparition. Looking through the small viewfinder, I thought I had failed. But when I was able to see the photograph on a large monitor, I was shocked to see what was in the trees to the right of the house. So take a look at the third photograph of the house and see if you can spot the cadre of apparitions that are on page 23 to the right of the house—another collective?

Figure 23: Here is the Ludwell Tenement, with a spherical apparition in the backyard. Could this apparition be one of the Revolutionary War soldiers who died from his wounds after being brought back to Williamsburg from the Battle of Yorktown? Notice the Red Balloon-like apparition is still in front of the house, right in the center gable window on the roof. There's also a small, bright yellow orb at the bottom of the right gable window.

Figure 23a: I took this photo of the roof of the Ludwell Tenement just a few seconds after tFigure 23, and as always, whenever the apparition sees the camera pointed at the roof, it makes a move to escape—here it is leaving the scene.

Figure 23b: A close-up shot of the bottom part of the Ludwell Tenement apparition.

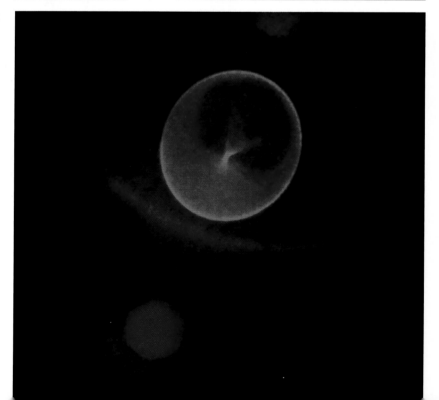

Figure 23c: This photo, taken a few months later of the Ludwell Tenement, has something that is concealed in the tree to the right. Compare this photo to the very first one of the Ludwell Tenement. Notice how the apparition appeared behind the house and tree in the first photo is now right out in front of the house observing me.

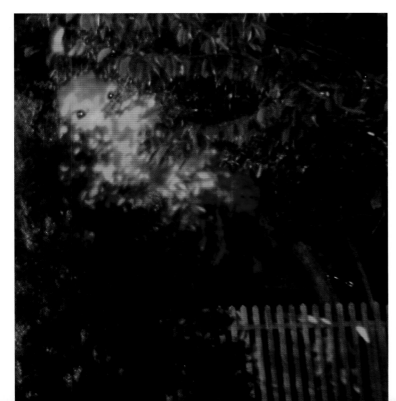

Figure 23d: This is a crop of Figure 23c, possibly showing a group of Revolutionary War soldiers leaving the woods behind the Ludwell Tenement to make an appearance out front. If you did not look closely, you may have missed these apparitions to the right of the house. Notice how that although there is one large, dominant face (perhaps their leader?), there are several others in the mix, including some behind the fence.

CHAPTER TWENTY-FOUR

Secretary's Office

(OF THE CAPITOL)

Nearsighted in Two Different Realities

History

Although the Capitol is a reconstructed building, the Secretary's Office, where all court and governmental records were kept, is an original eighteenth-century building. It is the oldest building of its kind in the Western Hemisphere. After the Capitol burned down in January of 1747, the secretary of the colony asked for leave in April to draw up a bill for the financing of a building for the preservation of public records—a building that was made as fireproof as possible given the technology of the time. The bill was passed and the construction bill was paid late in 1748 for the Secretary's Office, which would keep all public records until 1780 when the Capital was moved to Richmond. On the inside, plaster was laid on brick and as little wood as possible was used, and fireplaces were constructed to prevent downdrafts from sending sparks into the rooms. After 1780, the office became a Court of Admiralty for a while, then it became the residence for the headmaster of a grammar school that was held in the former Capital building. Next it became a female academy, and later it was converted back into a residence before Colonial Williamsburg purchased it and restored it. Have you ever heard the expression about anything to do with government, "It's tied up in red tape"? That expression comes from the practice in colonial times of tying up volumes of public records with a red, ribbon-like material; now anything that gets bogged down in formal government process has the moniker "tied up in red tape."

Ghost Story & Insights

There is a ghost story associated with this building when it was used as a home in the twentieth century. The daughter of the family that lived there was very near-sighted (myopic). She had a very strict, over-protective father, and she met a young man at her home whom she fell in love with, but was forbidden to pursue her love. Evidently it was very unbecoming of a woman to wear glasses then, and the girl was very self-conscious about wearing them. One day the two young lovers conspired to run away together. The self-conscious woman left home without her glasses, wanting to look as appealing as she possibly could for her boyfriend. Because of her poor vision, she did not see a carriage coming and stepped right in front of it, ending her life as we know it. She continues on with life as only she knows it—and occupies her former home. The irony of it all is that in her efforts to flee the confines of this home the young woman died and remains to this day imprisoned in the house that she tried to escape.

This building has a new, different-shaped apparition: an oval with a bright spot (I wonder if that's where it processes thoughts?) attached to a second shape that is a cross between an oval and an octagon. Although this does not look like the other Red Super Cell apparitions, it is red, large, and has the Yellow Umbrella to the far right. Another anomaly: the large red portion of the apparition rests on the building rather than hovering over it, and the Yellow Umbrella—which usually rests on the building—

instead is over a small graveyard to the right of the building. What's also different about the large apparition on the roof is that it doesn't seem to be a guardian of the building like all of the others. It did not move towards me like the others to see what I was doing, but remained immobile on the roof. Perhaps the spirit still believes that it is nearsighted . . .

Figure 24: Here is the Secretary's Office of the Colony of Virginia, with a very different-looking apparition that seems to be at rest on the rooftop. It remained immobile while I was there, unlike other apparitions that would move closer to me to see what I was doing. Not the conjoining grey orbs floating by.

I fully expected to see more paranormal activity here because of the small graveyard to the right of the Secretary's Office—based on all of the apparitions at the Bruton Parish Church. (I know that it is not nearly as big as the church's graveyard, but I expected to see more than this. This apparition is very difficult to photograph, and it's rare that I get anything over this building.) After many attempts, I was able to capture the elongated face of a young woman in two windowpanes. Is it the myopic young woman who tried to escape? Is the apparition on top of the building responsible for projecting the face in the window?

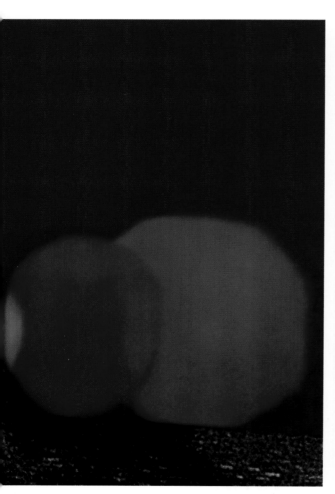

Figure 24a: Here Figure 24 cropped to show only the large, segmented apparition that appears motionless on the roof of the Secretary's Office, right next to the Capital Building.

Figure 24b: Perhaps the near-sighted female who was run over by a carriage? The face looks elongated, as if it's stretched to fill both windowpanes.

CHAPTER TWENTY-FIVE

Orrell House

The Itinerant Poltergeist

There is no written eighteenth-century data on this house, and, therefore, no evidence that tailor Thomas Orrell ever owned it. But if they would just change the "e" in Orrell to an "i," they have proof that a John Orrill owned the house (in accounting books dating from 1806 to 1808). Other than that, there is no compelling history about the property. However, take note of something interesting that's floating overhead: a number of orbs shaped like hexagons—ghosts' favorite geometric shape.

The Orrell House has an itinerant poltergeist whose on-again off-again activity, reported by one family that stayed here, includes turning the water on (more than a few times to irritate the guests), removing a glass from its wrapping and shattering it on the bathroom floor, and using toilet paper like a Halloween prank—only decorating the inside bathroom instead of the outside. Yes, this ghost prefers to wreak havoc in the bathroom for some reason, and evidently only with certain families. Perhaps the ghost saw someone in that family that reminded him or her of a person in their lifetime that really angered the itinerant wraith. Possibly this ghost travels to an alternate dimension or reality and only returns to vandalize the bathroom because of a certain catalyst. By the way, this home is a lodging house that you can book during your stay in Williamsburg—what are you waiting for? Do you have what it takes to bring out the ire of this wrathful wraith?

Figure 25: Here is the hexagon-laden Orrell House.

Figure 25a: Here Figure 25 is cropped to see all the hexagon-shaped orbs over the Orrell House.

Figure 25b: This classic white showed up in the side downstairs window in an usual move: Ghosts, for the most part, try to remain concealed, and not look me right in the eye.

Figure 25d: This unusual apparition, about the size of a softball, was resting on the handrail on the outside of the house.

Figure 25c: The photo shows a couple of the occupants of the Orrell House; the partial face on the bottom looks rather angry—perhaps he's the on-again-off-again poltergeist responsible for wrecking the bathroom.

CHAPTER TWENTY-SIX

Timson House

A Different Type of Red Super Cell?

One of the oldest structures in Williamsburg, successful York County planter William Timson built this one-room house in 1716. Timson's tenure in this structure was short-lived; he sold it in 1717 to tailor James Shields. Shields lived at the house until 1745; he sold the house to James Wray, who used the house as a rental property until the Revolution. Although the home has had no residents that were famous or infamous, it has a very deep red-colored orb that is very different from anything we've seen so far. There are no ghost stories that I know of, nevertheless the ghosts are here . . .

Figure 26: Here is the Timson House with a very deep red-colored orb hovering near the chimney.

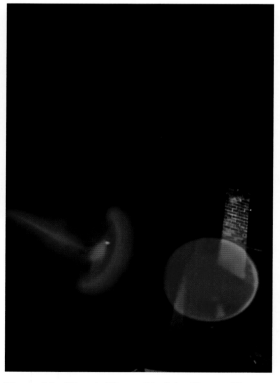

Figure 26a: Here is Figure 26 of the Timson House apparition cropped to see some unique features not seen before.

Figure 26b: The side of the Timson House has a similar Red Super Cell at the front, but attached to the light on the side.

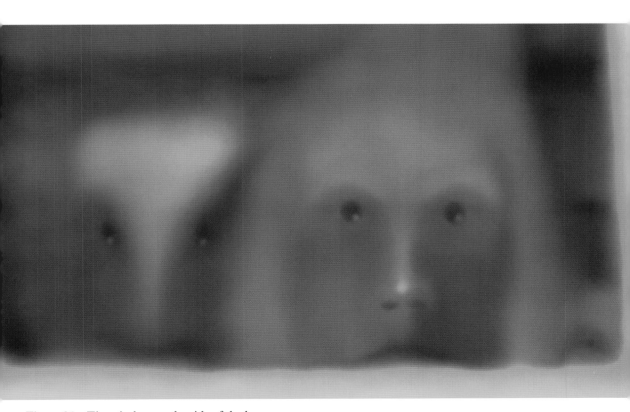

Figure 26c: The window on the side of the house also had a couple of faces—a classic white and a face that looks right at home in the eighteenth century, complete with what looks like a wig.

CHAPTER TWENTY-SEVEN

The [Slaves'] Quarters

Ghosts . . . or Aliens?

This very small structure is simply called the "Quarter," but what Colonial Williamsburg really means is the slaves' quarters. This one very tiny lodging for slaves boasts quite a huge gathering of apparitions; not only what you can see on the outside, but also the faces in the windows. My first photograph of this building produced an array of apparitions, I'm not sure if a cloud is in the mix or not, but it almost looks like two glowing eyes in the sky. On this page you will see the partial face that I found in the gable window from this photo. But if that doesn't tweak your interest, then perhaps the ghost in the side window that looks like an alien might . . .

Figure 27: Slaves' Quarters.

Figure 27a: This is the partial face that I found in the gable window from Figure 27, with the contrast turned up a bit.

Figure 27b: Here is quite a large gathering of apparitions over the Slaves' Quarters; it makes you wonder how many people were actually forced to live in this tiny house.

Figure 27d: Here is a crop to show the face in the top pane of the window with the contrast turned up even more; it was quite small in comparison to the bottom two. It looks more like a baby alien than a ghost.

Figure 27c: The window on the side of the Slaves' Quarters had several apparitions of the ghostly kind; in other words a kind of white face with dark eyespots, a nose structure, and possibly a mouth (one of the three doesn't have a mouth). The one at the top is quite small—it's the smallest that I've seen so far in the windows. The one in the middle will probably remind you of the one at the jail. The one at the bottom has the eyespot, but no other feature. I'm going to enlarge the first two to let you see them better (Figures 27d and 27e). I'm curious as to why the bottom two, just like the one at the jail in the bottom window, would only show half of its face. According to the psychic that accompanied me one night, these apparitions would look out the window with only half their face, and then quickly move back into the darkness of the room (she could actually see them—but I could not). I must have been lucky to catch all three looking out in this photo. (As you can probably tell, the contrast of this photograph was turned up enough to wash out any detail in the wood separating the individual panes of glass.)

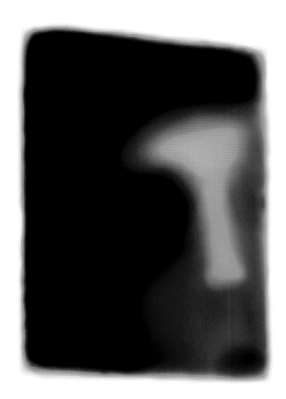

Figure 27e: This is the face that reminds me of the one at the jail; like the one at the jail it will only show half its face in the window. After looking at the very tiny apparition in Figure 27d, whose face has a dark half and a light half, I wonder if they only have enough energy to light up half their face (or their equivalent of a face). Also, they line their faces up so that you can't really see the mouth. But do they even have a mouth? Do they need a mouth? We have a mouth to eat food and to vocalize words—they can do neither. I'm sure the nose structure is not functional either; maybe it's just a façade to let people know they are there.

I thought you would like to see some additions to that cast of previously seen orbs, apparitions, ghosts, and alien ghosts, starting off with a ghostly white typical of the classic Halloween ghost cartoon. Finally there are two, or maybe several faces that made an appearance in the downstairs window that look less than angelic. You may recall Part I that faces have a habit of appearing in windows with an unusual eye feature: one eye is dark and one eye is light. Both of the clearest apparitions have this characteristic that I find over and over again in the faces that I have captured trapped in the windowpanes. I don't know what the significance is in this alternate reality, but I do know that the dark eye has an eerie, if not menacing look that may reveal a second side to the personality behind the face. What may be the homes for the living seem to be the prisons for those that are dead. Iron bars and doors may not trap them, but it's quite obvious that they cannot leave—bound by invisible bars that we cannot see or touch.

The Richard Crump House

The house next door (the Richard Crump House) had its own cast of bizarre, if not unsavory characters in the backyard looking over the picket fence as if they were keenly interested in what I was doing. A man that we know next to nothing about owned the house right next to the Slaves' Quarters at one time. Perhaps it's

Figure 27f: Looking through the opening in the drapes, this looks like one of Casper's friends, complete with the wispy top.

Figure 27g: This apparition in the side window of the Slave Quarters looks a little devilish: red with something like the appearance of horns. The skull is something that normally is not what you see on the curtains, but then again what is normal in this alternate reality?

because he was not involved in government, or in the Revolutionary War, or was fabulously wealthy like everybody else in Williamsburg. Crump is listed on the tax records as holding the property from 1785 to 1794, after which he seems to disappear into the annals of time. Crump was one of many owners of this property, but by far I think one of the most interesting owners was Zizi. This person with a most interesting name was a woman described as "a free person of color." Although she was a "person of color" she had no qualms about keeping slaves—she owned three of them. I find it curious that Zizi not only could afford a house in Williamsburg but also had slaves; I bet there

is an interesting story behind what little we know from tax records.

Besides the woman with the exotic name, I found something else interesting about this property: a collection of curious apparitions looking over the fence at me while I photographed the slaves' quarters. I have no idea if they have exotic names, but they do have exotic—or should I say bizarre—faces that may pique your interest. I don't know if they know what a camera is, but they seem anxious to make a ragtag appearance either to be seen or to be photographed. Some have missing or incomplete facial features; perhaps they are still learning how to re-create themselves with light . . .

Figure 27h: Two or more characters showed up in the downstairs windowpane on the side of the tiny house when the blinds were not down. Notice that once again we have the light eye/dark eye effect, which can be a bit unnerving to some viewers . . . not to mention the guy on the left is missing his lips!

CHAPTER TWENTY-EIGHT

Ewing House

Which One Is Ebenezer, and What's with the Eyes?

A map made around the year 1790 indicates this property belonged to the Ewing family; a will from 1795 indicates Ebenezer Ewing owned the house and willed it to his son, Thomas. Besides the common spherical apparition appearing over the roof, there are a couple of characters that appear in the windows of the Ewing house that are more compelling than the lackluster history of the home. The first is a rather stern-looking fellow; I thought in tribute to Charles Dickens, I would name this fellow Ebenezer; it just seems appropriate. The second character in the window of this home must have a sense of humor—it's the first time I ever had a gap-mouthed apparition show his tongue to me, and the last character has a normal face, but the background is so bizarre: eyes are everywhere!

In this chapter I explain my editing process, but I would like to state several things. Although I try to only use the faces that show up the clearest, many times faces are distorted and out of proportion (like in the backyard of the Richard Crump House), particularly if they try to appear in two windowpanes rather than one—they become disproportionately elongated. Secondly, it is necessary to turn up the contrast, so much so that faces will sometimes look more like cartoons or caricatures than real faces; just try it with one of your own. Finally, I realize that these photos are controversial, and no matter what I do, say, or offer as proof, some people will not believe. For the rest of you, here are the faces of the Ewing House and a glimpse into my editing process.

Figure 28: For the first time, I have captured a spherical apparition without the requisite Red Balloon a few feet below. In its place, on the second-floor center window, I found the apparition on Figure 28a.

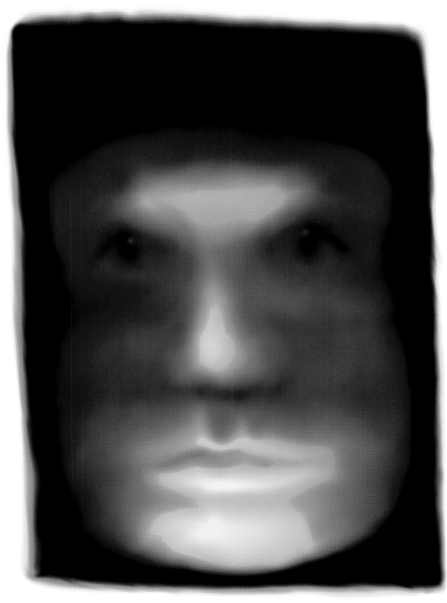

Figure 28a: Here's the first of three cropped photographs of the Ewing House; two of the three came from Figure 28. What's unusual about this first crop is that this apparition took the place of the "Red Balloon" part of the apparition, which is the first time I've seen that happen. The Red Balloon-like part of the spherical apparition has accompanied every one of the spheres up till this one. Instead, I found this stern-looking character up in the central gable window; he looks like an "Ebeneezer" to me.

Here is a crop from the bottom left-hand windowpanes—looking right at me. I think that this apparition has a sense of humor; it is showing me his tongue! He looks more like a caricature than a ghost, and he's the first apparition-face to take up more than one windowpane—but not the last.

Evolution of the Editing Process

This is an attempt to demonstrate the editing process, so that I'm not accused of creating faces with Photoshop tricks:

Step 1: Crop the face out of the original photo. At this point, the face is usually only about a half inch.

Step 2: Increase it to a working size (about 3 inches), increase the contrast to bring out the features.

Step 3: Depixalize the face so that it does not look grainy, add more contrast as necessary, then increase the photo to its final size.

Figure 28b: Step 1.

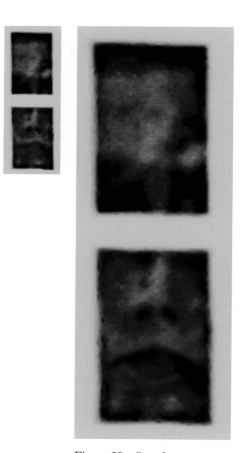
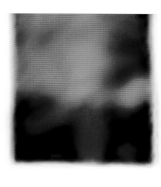

Figure 28c: Step 2.   Figure 28d: Step 3.

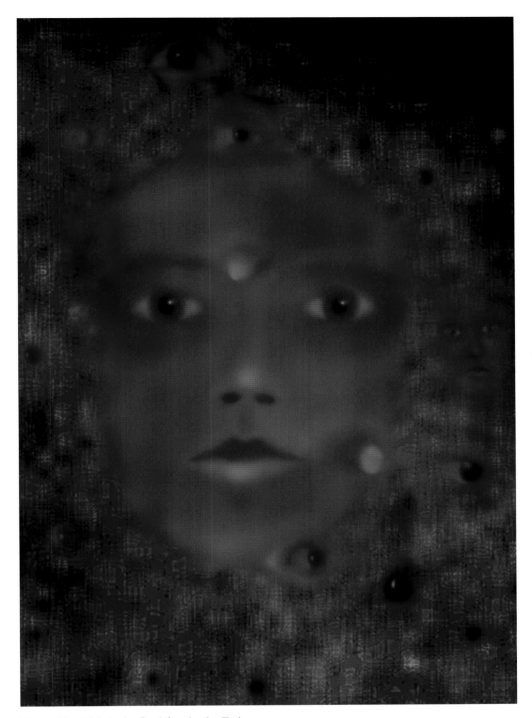

Figure 28e: This is the final face in the Ewing House (that I'm aware of), and it appears as if more than one spirit wanted to be a part of the appearance. This is one of the most bizarre faces that I've captured yet . . . eyes everywhere, even the small dark spots, when magnified, look like eyes. Did you notice the small face?

CHAPTER TWENTY-NINE

Benjamin Waller House

Intimidation in a Window Near You!

History

Benjamin Waller was a respected and influential lawyer; he studied law using Sir John Randolph's library, and he eventually taught law to George Wythe (Thomas Jefferson's mentor and teacher). The man was definitely self-motivated—teaching himself to be a lawyer without the help of an organized institution or learned professors. (By the way, one other important figure that was influential in the movement to independence did the very same thing—Patrick Henry.) Waller was also a land developer, a civil servant, and a community leader. Some of the positions he held are clerk and burgess for James City County, recorder of Williamsburg, vestryman of Bruton Parish Church, and judge of the Court of Admiralty. This property was purchased sometime before 1750 by Waller and it remained in the family for over a century. I wonder if that means that the very bright dominant spirit overhead is a Waller? Some apparitions that look rather ominous hang out in the first floor far right window; are they members of the Waller family too? Or are they buried in the graveyard out back and have decided to occupy the closest residence to their gravesite?

Insights

I usually look for evidence of an overhead apparition before shooting at specific windows. Most buildings will have a dominant spirit hovering over the home or building or a "Red Super Cell," but in ghostography, there are always exceptions—the Peyton Randolph House and the Gaol do not have dominant spirits or even Red Super Cells overhead, just the grey orbs. The Waller House had one of the brightest Spherical Torches that I've seen over a residence, comparable to the Bowden-Armstead or St. George Tucker Houses. The first night that I found classic white apparitions (you know, the classic appearance of a white "Halloween ghost"), the window blinds were opened on the bottom floor. If the blinds are drawn or the shutters are closed, I usually get nothing when I photograph the window. But like I just said, there are always exceptions, and the Waller House is one. The second time I took window shots of this house, the blinds were drawn and I did not expect to get much of anything. I was shocked to find that between the blinds and the window, little points of light were moving around as if they were drawing a face in the windowpane! In another window, glowing orange orbs of light (not reflections from artificial light) were creating several tiny faces in the lower panes of the windows. These apparitions were on a mission to be noticed!

Figure 29: The Benjamin Waller has a very bright dominant spirit overhead, and quite a gathering of other apparitions in the first floor far right window.

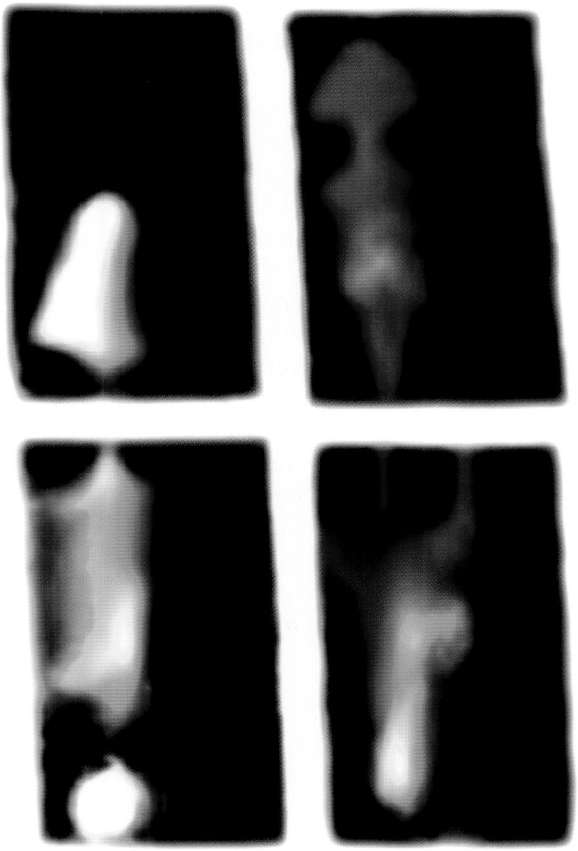

Figure 29a: Figure 29 has been cropped to show a window full of intimidating faces on the first floor far right; are they all former occupants of this house, or are they buried in the graveyard behind this domicile?

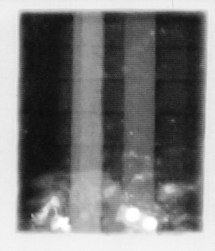

Figure 29b: Here are the window shots of the Benjamin Waller House with the blinds drawn. Usually, these kinds of shots will show no paranormal activity, but here are the exceptions in the first-floor windows. Can you see any tiny faces in the orb fireworks below?

Figure 29c: In this photo, you can see tiny points of light moving as if they are drawing the faces.

Figure 29d: Here is a close-up of the face on 29c left, which is much clearer than the one on the right.

The Cross and the Catwoman

This house has no shortage of paranormal activity, and here are several new apparitions, including a close-up of the Spherical Torch, which has an unusual feature that I did not see in the first photograph and that I've never seen before: at the point where you would usually see the torch-like light or flame, you see what resembles a cross with a circle around it. I don't know if this has any religious significance or not. Check back to page 143 to see the first photograph of this apparition; it's not nearly as well defined as this photo.

Figure 29e: This house has no shortage of paranormal activity, and here are several new apparitions, including a close-up of the Spherical Torch, which has an unusual feature that I did not see in the first photograph and that I've never seen before: at the point where you would usually see the torch-like light or flame, you see what resembles a cross with a circle around it. I don't know if this has any religious significance or not. The first photo of this apparition is on page 143.

Figure 29f: For some reason, this woman's likeness is very catlike; is it the angry eyes?

Figure 29g: Here are three different faces from three different windowpanes at the Benjamin Waller House. It's as if each ghost is allocated one and only one windowpane to show their face, and each apparition is a different view of their face. But the rest of the face does not bleed over into another pane, which makes me believe that it is like a hologram created by the entity; perhaps they are unable to create the whole facial likeness from their former lives. On the bottom left you can see an incomplete face forming as well as an ephemeral classic white above it; does the ghost need more time to complete the face? Does it lack the energy to recreate the remainder? Or is it just unable to finish the likeness? It makes me think that recreating a likeness of their former selves is a learned skill—otherwise wouldn't they all be doing it? Wouldn't you?

CHAPTER THIRTY

Robert Nicolson House

One Dominant and Two Submissive ... but Jack, Is That Your Relative?

History & a Ghost Story

Tailor and merchant Robert Nicolson built this house sometime between 1751 and 1753, and business must have been good because he added the left-hand portion around 1766. Nicolson was boarding lodgers as early as 1755; one particular boarder ran an add in the *Virginia Gazette* offering to teach "ladies and gentlemen" how to play keyboard instruments like the organ, harpsichord, and spinet. His name was Cuthbert Ogle, and some say that he is one of the entities haunting this place. Ogle fell ill soon after he arrived, and his untimely death must have given him a sense of unfinished business. The story is that Cuthbert continues to open the front door and looks out down the street to see if he has any customers coming. Obviously, from the photo below, you can see that the front door is not open, but at least three apparitions are present on the roof and seem to be in possession of this home. I have never seen three spherical apparitions on one small residence before—two of which are leaning to the side in tandem as if they are twins, both submissive to the dominant spirit overhead. As you will see in the subsequent photos, there are a lot more ghosts than one itinerant musician ogling at me from the confines of the Nicolson House.

Figure 30: Three Spherical Torches reside on top of the Robert Nicolson House.

Figure 30a: Here is Figure 30 cropped to show the unusual group of spherical apparitions: It appears as if one is dominant and the other two (twins?) are submissive and laying on their sides.

Figure 30b: This photo was taken several months later of the back of the Whetherburn Tavern, but I had to add it here to show the same anomaly: A Spherical Torch apparition with two additional ones (very close together) bent over to the side as if in submission. Perhaps this is less of an anomaly and more demonstrates that there is a pecking order even in alternate realities . . . By the way, this October full moon was a very active period for all the apparitions.

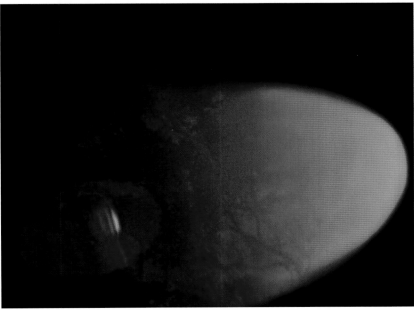

Figure 30c: Here is a cropped view of another photograph taken from the side of the Robert Nicolson house that reveals something a little different from the other apparitions you've seen so far. I don't know if this is one whole or two separate apparitions.

Figure 30d: A strange collage of unsavory faces
from the Robert Nicolson House; so which one is
Cuthbert, and who are some of other miscreants?

Figure 30e: Is this Cuthbert, or perhaps Robert Nicolson?
It reminds me of another Nicolson: Jack . . .

CHAPTER THIRTY-ONE

Dr. Barraud House

The Doctor Is In?

Either apothecary owner William Carter or blacksmith James Anderson erected the building as rental property in the 1760s or 1770s; the exact date is not known. But the man the home is named after is Dr. Philip Barraud, who bought the home in 1785. Following his service in the Revolutionary War, he studied medicine at the University of Edinburgh. Upon his return to America, he was hired as a "visiting physician" at the Public Hospital from 1795 until he became director of the Norfolk Marine Hospital in 1799. In 1801, Barraud sold the house to Anna Byrd, a widow, who proceeded to use it as a boarding house.

For the longest time, I could find nothing paranormal here, and I had doubts that this original home would be included in the book. Then one day, for whatever reason, the wraiths revealed their presence to me, the most intriguing being what appears to be a female head in the front window with a classic white in the windowpane beneath that looks more like a sheet billowing in the wind. Now I know where the idea came from to make a Halloween ghost costume: Just cut two holes in a sheet and throw it over your head.

Figure 31: I finally captured a dominant spirit hanging out at the chimney. If you look at the bottom left side, you will see a yellow orb on the picket fence; a crop and enlargement will reveal something more . . .

Figure 31a: Here is the crop of Figure 31 to see more than just a splotch of yellow light on a picket fence to the left of the house. The light resembles a cross and I hope you can see the face on the right that is partially covered by the cross. Notice the partial face on the left of the cross-shaped light. (You can see one eye and a nostril to the lower left.)

Figure 31b: Here is the cropped photograph of the roof of the Dr. Barraud House showing the spherical apparition up close. Notice that it has a blue orb and some extra shapes accompanying the Red Balloon . . . and the torch seems to be burning brightly.

Figure 31c: One of the front windows has an identifiable face and a classic white that more closely resembles an octopus than a ghost.

Figure 31d: One of the faces in the Dr. Barraud House has some extra eyes . . . perhaps the face or one of the eyes belongs to the good doctor.

CHAPTER THIRTY-TWO

Chiswell-Bucktrout House

The Lady Is . . . in the Tree?

James City County records were burned during the Civil War; so the year the Chiswell-Bucktrout House was built can only be approximated at 1764. Colonel John Chiswell, another prosperous man and member of the Virginia House of Burgesses (was every homeowner in Colonial Williamsburg a *colonel* and wealthy?), owned this home till 1766, when he was arrested for killing a Scottish merchant, a man who he called a "fugitive rebel, a villain who came to Virginia to cheat and defraud men of their property, and a Presbyterian fellow..." He was bailed out by three friends from Williamsburg. (Remember John Blair? You will read about his second friend, William Byrd soon; the third friend was Presley Thornton, someone we haven't discussed.) His other problem: this home was part of a dowry given to his son-in-law, who died owing the state a great deal of money. That meant the home would be put up on auction to recover that money. It seems that Chiswell did not believe that his trial would end well, because he died at his home before it took place. The cause of John Chiswell's death: nervous fits owing to constant uneasiness of the mind, "Notwithstanding this he is believed to have committed suicide." Now this home is not an original eighteenth-century home, but was reconstructed on the original foundation, and the place is said to be haunted.

Later owners of the house and the property behind it were the Bucktrouts, a family that has been Williamsburg morticians for years, and they still have a funeral home just a few miles from Colonial Williamsburg. Somewhere behind this home is an *extensive* unmarked pauper graveyard that archeologists have promised to one day locate and study. Williamsburg's poor were laid to rest here in the 1800s and early 1900s; who knows what effect that has on the paranormal activity at this house. But in one photo you will see four rather unclear faces that are checking me out from behind a shrub in the backyard.

Colonial Williamsburg uses this house to lodge tourists, and like several other homes in this book, there are not a lot of specifics about the paranormal activity. Some guests do not believe in ghosts, and others are afraid that their sanity will be questioned if they speak of hauntings and specters. Those not afraid to speak up have said that spirits touching them have awakened them out of a sound sleep; others have said that they have heard disembodied voices. I did not find a dominant spirit over the house itself, but I did find quite a bit of paranormal activity in the two trees in front of the house and streaking apparitions on the right side, as well as more than a few faces in the windows and a first that you will see on page 157.

Figure 32: Chiswell-Bucktrout House has more than a Red Super Cell in the trees, but you have to look really close . . . see the close-up on Figure 32a.

Figure 32a: The right side of the house has a plethora of streaking apparitions, and I found four faces staring at me from behind a shrub in the backyard when I magnified the photograph.

Figure 32b: This was a surprise and a first—the apparition of a woman in the tree in front of the Chiswell-Bucktrout House. When I turned up the contrast to bring out her features, the greens turned to yellows, and so I had a slightly blurry, but fairly detailed portrait of a woman that was wealthy enough to afford makeup.

Figure 32c: Could this be Colonial John Chiswell, the man arrested for killing a Scottish merchant—who would later commit suicide to avoid going on trial for murder?

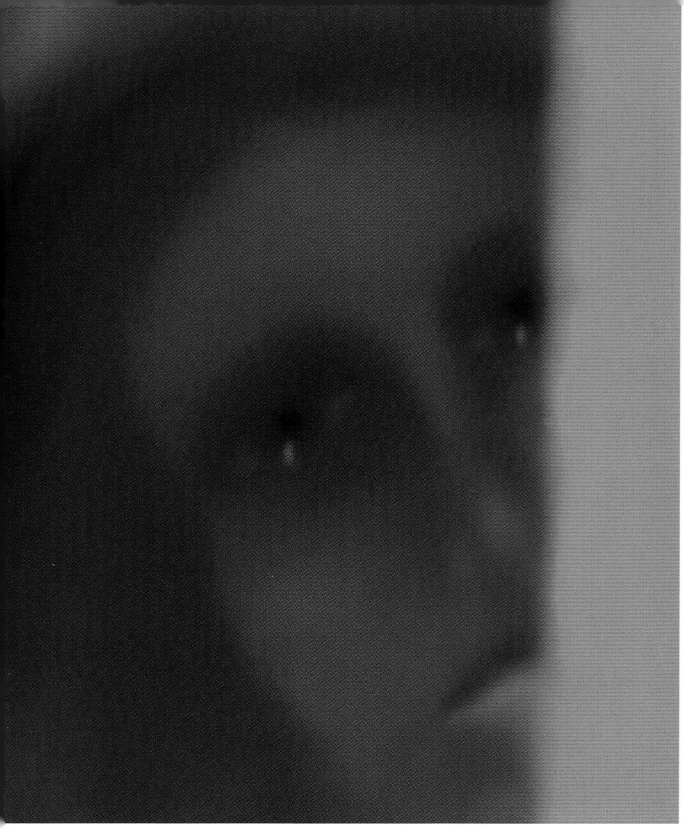

Figure 32f: Out of the many apparitions in the windows of the Chiswell-Bucktrout House, the females seem to be showing up the clearest; but there are a couple of classic whites lurking in the background.

Figure 32d and 32e: This female was inside the Chiswell-Bucktrout House, on one side of the window, with the much younger female on the next page on the other; mother and daughter?

Figure 32g: The two complacent male faces below are in stark contrast to the profound look of pain on the woman's face above them.

Figure 32h: These four faces watched me from behind a shrub in the backyard; they may be residents of the lost pauper cemetery somewhere behind the "Bucktrout Cottage."

CHAPTER THIRTY-THREE

William Finnie House

Displaced, Distraught, and Disturbed

What's Familiar in an Unfamiliar Reality?

I wanted to cover as many of the eighteenth-century homes and buildings as possible, but I only wanted to feature and do a close-up of those buildings that had apparitions with different, unusual features. Williamsburg is a hotbed for apparitions of all sorts, and it seems that everywhere I point my camera I pick up something. I can't tell you about all of the orbs in every photograph—there are so many. But many of them are very small, and so I chose only those that I thought would interest my readers. There are orbs everywhere—from tiny points of light smaller than a marble to ones that are monstrous, probably more than 100 feet in diameter (going by the size of the buildings they hover over). I was told that there are over several thousand people buried on or near the church grounds. (I know that seems like a lot, but many families occupy one lot—do you remember the story of Daniel Custis? Daniel, his son, and his daughter all occupy the same crypt next to the Bruton Parish Church). There have been many evenings when I've seen hundreds of orbs floating by different houses (remember the photo of the John Blair House or the Peyton Randolph House with the *orb blizzard*?). I have even seen tiny glowing orbs in the bushes surrounding some of the homes I've photographed making me wonder what these creatures were at one time. A better question is: What are the orbs that are gigantic and even larger than some of the buildings they hover over? It seems that I have more questions than answers, but this book is proof that something exists in the same space we do, and we have no idea how it exists, what sustains it, why it shape-shifts into all of these different sizes, shapes, and colors of light, and why it hangs around these buildings.

What I do know is that the apparitions are there, and I want a photographic record of every different kind, shape, and color. As I mentioned before, just like fingerprints and snowflakes, no two apparitions are exactly alike. What makes it more difficult is that they are shape-shifters, and so they will change their appearance in a matter of seconds—just go back and look at the five apparitions over the Wren Building, or turn back to look at the single apparition that hovers over the Geddy House. So what you will see in this part of the book are the remaining homes and buildings that have similar-looking apparitions to the ones that you have already seen, with minor, individual differences of course—and of course the faces. Where there is interesting, even compelling history, I've included that, too. So here they are, starting with one of my favorite eighteenth century houses, the William Finnie House.

William Finnie House

Labeled the "handsomest house in town" by St. George Tucker (see Chapter 2), the William Finnie House looks very different from most of the homes seen so far. William Finnie, quartermaster general in the Revolutionary War, lived here with his family from the 1770s to the mid 1780s. Colonial Williamsburg labels the home's design as a precursor to a classical influence that would later dominate American architecture. Judge James Sample, also a professor of law at the College of William and Mary, bought the home in 1800. After Judge Sample, the house has had a plethora of owners, so there is no telling which occupants from the house's past still claims the home in death . . .

Figure 33a: The William Finnie House is a hotbed for paranormal activity: Look at the very large orb coming from the top left, as well as the huge orb on the ground in the bottom left of the photograph (it's not very bright or well-defined) that is almost as large as the house itself—what on earth is that? William Finnie House; Classical Design, Classically Haunted.

Figure 33b: The Finnie House has what looks like a Spherical Torch with a different look, but upon closer examination you will see that it is very close to a Yellow Unbrella from another apparition. This is one of the more beautifully colored and designed apparitions—see the close-up on the next page.

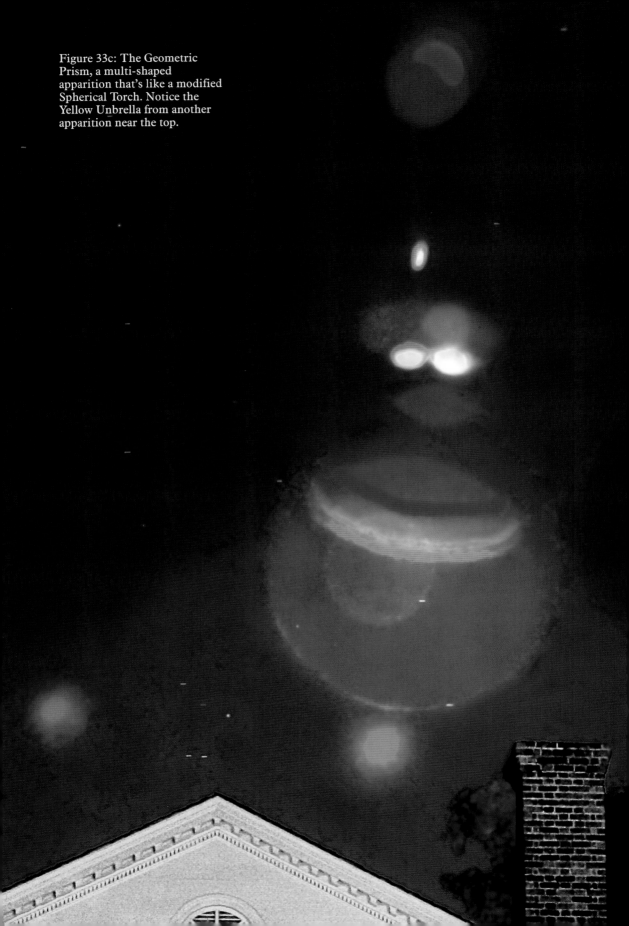

Figure 33c: The Geometric Prism, a multi-shaped apparition that's like a modified Spherical Torch. Notice the Yellow Unbrella from another apparition near the top.

A Ghost's Nightmare

There is one thing that you can do to a ghost that appears to make them feel displaced, distraught, sometimes angry, confused, and anxious: repair or remodel their residence. When I saw the scaffolding going up around the Finney House I saw it as an opportunity to capture increased paranormal activity. One of my reluctant psychics came with me on this particular night, although she preferred to stay in the car. She nevertheless picked up on the emotions being projected by all of the Finney phantoms, with the feeling of displacement being the strongest of all. Up until this point, I was never able to capture an actual face in the window of the William Finney House; now I had my pick of a plethora of different visages—as always, I chose the clearest and most detailed of the lot to put in this book.

One point about this whole scenario made me stop and think: Are ghosts attached to the building as a whole, or just one particular part of it? What happens if the ghost is attached to a specific board, window, or door, and that piece is discarded during the repair? Does the ghost go to the landfill, or is its link to this dimension forever broken? Is this why they are so anxious?

Figure 33d: The repair of the William Finney House has disturbed and displaced all of Finney's phantoms.

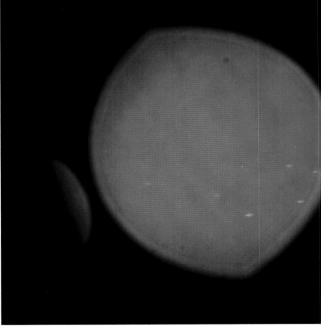

Figure 33f: Besides the three orbs that showed up near the separate kitchen building, the close-up of the one above was to the far right of the main house.

Figure 33e: A new kind of orb showed up at the Finney Kitchen; it's a misshapen orb with a light violet color—it reminds me of a lemon.

 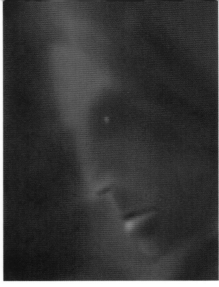 

Figure 33g: This woman appeared in a windowpane looking up at something that I could not see.

Figure 33h: But in the same window, the next row over, this man was looking down at something that I likewise could not see.

Figure 33i: For the first time, a detailed face is accompanied by a set of stacking apparitions.

 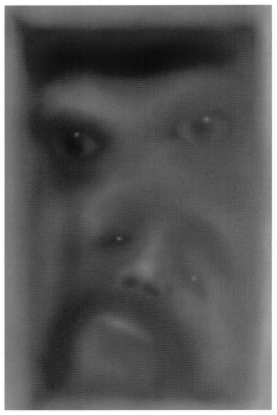

Figure 33j: A not quite as well defined face tries to appear through a set of blinds at the William Finney House.

Figure 33k: Two sets of eyes watch me—the light eye/dark eye characteristic of many of these apparitions has become a classic trait of this alternate reality—I wish I knew what it meant. Could it have something to do with good and evil?

CHAPTER THIRTY-FOUR

Thomas Nelson House

Does Williamsburg's Oldest House Have Its Oldest Wraiths?

Built in 1695, this is the oldest dwelling in Williamsburg and one of the oldest frame houses in Virginia. The home's most famous owner was Thomas Nelson Jr., one of the signers of the Declaration of Independence, commander of the Virginian forces at the Battle of Yorktown, and the man who succeeded Thomas Jefferson to the governorship of Virginia. One of the best stories about the Revolutionary War has to do with the Battle of Yorktown and Thomas Nelson Jr.: Back during the Revolutionary War (and the Civil War, too) it was common practice for an invading army to requisition houses, food, firewood, horses, and just about anything else that they could scavenge from the populace. Officers, particularly commanders, would stay in the best homes (recall the Robert Carter House)—and of course people of wealth would have the means to escape the occupation by moving to safety. Cornwallis was a member of the British nobility, and was quite used to being surrounded by wealth. So out in the field, whenever possible, Cornwallis would choose the very best accommodations when setting up his headquarters—and his enemies knew that.

Thomas Nelson Jr. was himself a wealthy man—the wealthiest in all of Yorktown, and he had the largest Georgian mansion on the bluff overlooking the York River. (He, like other wealthy men of his time, also had this townhouse in Virginia's capital: Williamsburg.) Nelson, and all of the other officers in the combined Continental and French Armies, knew Cornwallis' propensities. British Commander Cornwallis had set up his headquarters in Nelson's house in Yorktown—a house built like a fortress, with thick walls made of red brick. Nelson was the commander of the Virginia Militia, and rather than worry about saving his mansion, he put the war effort ahead of his own interests and told his men to aim the cannons at his own house! (More about this in my next book!) In fact, you can visit Nelson's House today and still see some of the cannon balls embedded into the brick walls. Nelson's Williamsburg House has had many owners throughout the years since this Revolutionary War icon owned it, and there is no telling who occupies the alternate reality of the Nelson House.

I photographed this house many times and came up with nothing, but finally I captured an elusive but quite elegant apparition. I have related this same idea several times throughout this book, and it makes me wonder about these reality television shows searching for ghosts. They expect to stay one night and capture all of the paranormal activity the site has to offer—*it doesn't work that way!* From my experience, it takes multiple visits! I realize that they have budgets, television crews, and lots of expensive equipment—but that doesn't always bring out the spirits. Ghosts were people, and sometimes they have to get used to your presence before they reveal themselves. Like I have said before, I think that the dead are just as afraid of the living as we are of the dead. I have captured ghosts looking around corners, from behind or inside of shrubs, and often revealing only half of their faces when looking out the windows of the houses or buildings that they occupy. In fact, I have probably captured more apparitions in the periphery of my photographs than where I was aiming for.

At the Nelson House I was finally able to, after many tries, photograph a collection of recognizable faces that may have lived here at one time—perhaps even a Nelson or two.

Figure 34: Thomas Nelson's Williamsburg House— oldest in Williamsburg!

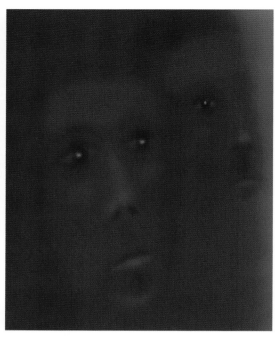

Figure 34b: Two faces look out from the oldest wooden structure in Williamsburg; could it be members of the Nelson family?

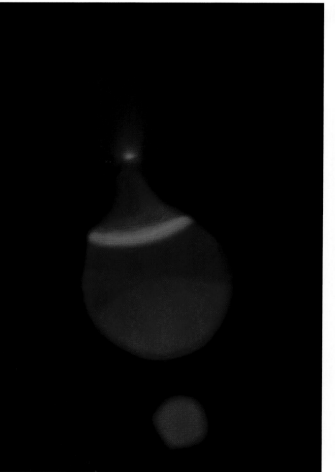

Figure 34a: Here is Figure 34 of the Thomas Nelson Jr. House cropped to show the very colorful apparition that after many attempts, I was finally able to capture.

Figure 34c: Another lonely face looks out forlornly from a windowpane in the Nelson House, appearing between the window blinds and the glass.

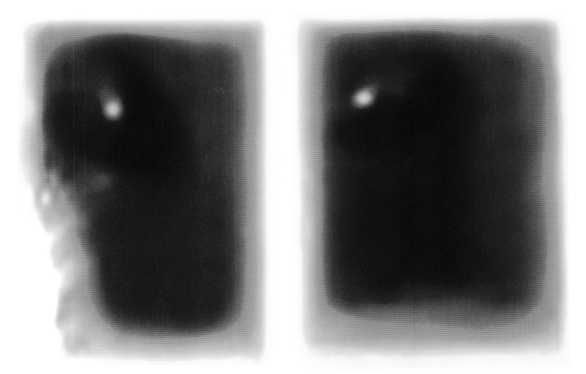

Figure 34d: A large pair of eyes look out from the same window just 2 panes up.

Figure 34e: As is so often the case, one ghost is able to appear as a recognizable face while its companion is only capable of appearing as a classic white.

CHAPTER THIRTY-FIVE

Lightfoot House

The Guardian Ghost of Presidents, Kings, and Dignitaries

Built sometime between 1730 and 1750; this house was believed to have been a tenement (rental) property for Philip Lightfoot III—you guessed it—another fabulously wealthy man from Caroline County. It may have been used as a commercial property, but it was renovated in 1750 into a townhouse of pretention and its present-day appearance. In 1962, it became the designated residence for all of Colonial Williamsburg's most distinguished guests, including Margaret Thatcher (an amazing woman that I was able to meet and hear speak at William and Mary), Anwar Sadat of Egypt, Indira Gandhi of India, King Olav V of Norway, and François Mitterand of France. It's

my understanding that President Ronald Reagan stayed here during the Economic Summit held in Williamsburg in the 1980s.

I wonder if all of these heads of state knew that they were not sleeping alone . . . other than the Spherical Torch that sits on the roof, there are a couple of characters in the Lightfoot House that might make guests uneasy. It's hard to find anyone in such a transient accommodation to admit to anything supernatural—let alone famous world leaders, so the stories about this house are not forthcoming. What is evident is that there are paranormal occupants in this beautiful house; all you have to do is look at the following pages!

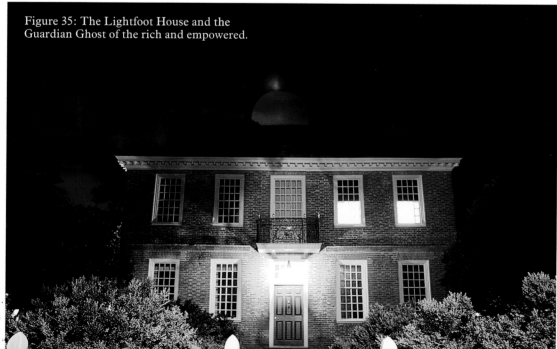

Figure 35: The Lightfoot House and the Guardian Ghost of the rich and empowered.

Figure 35a: This is the first paranormal presence that caught my attention on the night of a full moon in early March at the Lightfoot House.

Figure 35b: The second uninvited guest was much smaller and more difficult to see; the contrast button was able to bring him out a lot more. Just think, this man gets to stay with kings, queens, and heads of state! By the way, do you notice a third eye making an appearance to the left of his head?

CHAPTER THIRTY-SIX

William Byrd III House

For the Man Who Has Everything: Is Suicide the Only Answer?

History

William Byrd III was wealthy beyond most people's dreams, and yet he could have been the poster child for the expression "Money can't buy you happiness." Including the town home you are about to see in Colonial Williamsburg, he owned 179,000 acres, hundreds of slaves, mills, fisheries, vessels, warehouses, and a store. Oh, and did I mention one of the largest, most beautiful mansions in Virginia, overlooking the James River, called Westover? (Google or Bing it—you can still see it today.) Byrd studied law at Middle Temple, London, where he seems to have acquired a gambling problem. The man who seemed to have it all blew it all by both gambling and living outside his means—however extraordinary that was. In order to pay off his debts, his estate was taken control of by seven trustees, who began liquidating his holdings to pay back all of the money he owed. Since that didn't solve the problem, William decided on a more unconventional way to dig himself out of debt: he held a lottery, the prizes for which were to come from his estate at the falls of the James River.

It seems William's problems extended into his married life. He, like the vast majority of the people of his day, married into his social class: at the age of twenty he married Elizabeth Hill Carter; the Carters being another one of Virginia's enormously wealthy families. The couple had four sons and one daughter, and remained married until the same year that Byrd turned over his estate to the trustees. He repudiated his wife Elizabeth. (I know, it's the wording of the old records; its one of those eighteenth-century words that means he divorced her.) He sent his three eldest children to live with their aunt and uncle in England, dissolved his marriage, and joined the English army. From 1756 until 1761, Byrd took part in military campaigns from the Carolinas to Nova Scotia, and eventually succeeded George Washington as commander of the First Virginia Regiment. In the meantime, his wife Elizabeth, after writing many letters imploring the return of her husband, is believed to have committed suicide in 1760 (more on this in my next book). In that same year, he met a woman in Philadelphia who would become his second wife, and with whom he would have ten more children.

So William resigned from the military life and returned to civilian life with wife number two. He resumed his seat on the Governor's Council and resumed managing his huge holdings. But it seems that Byrd still had a huge amount of debt, and yet continued a lavish lifestyle until 1777 when he too, like his first wife, committed suicide at his Westover Plantation at the age of forty-eight. It's not known how much time Byrd spent in his townhome in Williamsburg, but from the photographs you can see that there are no brightly colored apparitions—just the large, ominous red apparitions on both sides of the house that seem to announce that happiness is not derived from wealth. The house was built in 1771, when Byrd bought it, and remained in his possession until his death in 1777.

Another owner of the home, Miss Gibbie Galt, likewise experienced hard times in this house due to the Civil War, which made paupers out of many Southern families.

The home today looks like it needs a few repairs, and sits isolated from the rest of Colonial Williamsburg in a parking lot across from the Williamsburg Hospital (CW's reconstructed asylum). Isolated too are the ghosts.

The busy road in front of this house makes it difficult to photograph, but I was finally able to capture a couple of Red Super Cells overhead and a couple of faces inside. To accomplish this I had to wait till late at night to photograph a couple of long-time residents of the Byrd Townhouse. Although unlikely William (who committed suicide at his Westover Plantation House), the first phantom face has the appearance of an eighteenth-century man—lacking facial hair and possibly wearing a long, curly wig; perhaps a previous or later owner. The second gentleman is likely from the nineteenth century, probably the Civil War era, because of his full beard—in vogue at the time for men.

Figure 36: The William Byrd III House is dominated by two large, ominous red orbs (the one on the left is similar to the Timson House apparition) on each side, with a few other orbs hovering nearby; there is a little bit of everything—if you look closely!

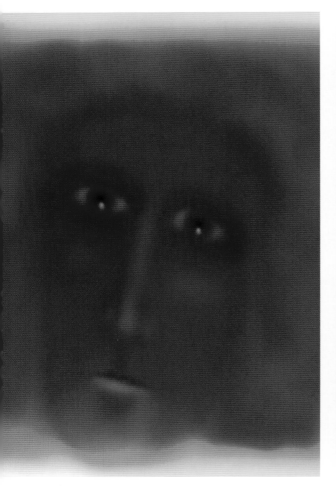

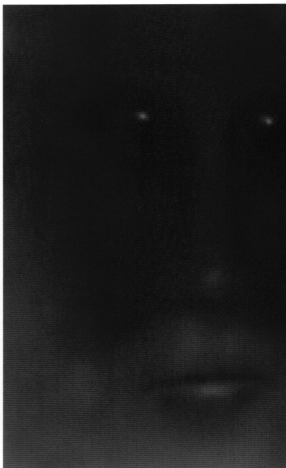

Figure 36a: This resident, without any facial hair and what seems like a long, curly wig that can only be afforded by the rich (making him a "bigwig"), is not likely William Byrd, but he is likely from the eighteenth century because of his appearance.

Figure 36b: Here's a fellow that's probably from the nineteenth century; with all that facial hair he's likely from the Civil War era.

CHAPTER THIRTY-SEVEN

Williamsburg Inn

Five Stars for the Afterlife

No, it's not an eighteenth-century building; it was finished and opened in 1937. It was designed in a neoclassical style in stark contrast to buildings in eighteenth-century Williamsburg. The Williamsburg Inn is the direct result of John D. Rockefeller's vision, giving meticulous attention to detail and bears the distinction of being the first hotel in America with central air-conditioning. No, I was not expecting to find anything over the building—it just looked like a great photograph. But I found something very similar to what I found over the Wren Building—except that the military order was missing—this looks more like a group of friends hanging out together. There were two bright Spherical Torches in the front, two slightly faded ones behind them, and to their right was a Red Super Cell. If they are not a group of friends, then perhaps this is a whole family that all met their end together in some tragic way. It makes me wonder if these apparitions are attached to the inn itself, or the land the inn is on. Are they former guests at the inn, or are they Native Americans, English colonists, Civil War soldiers, or slaves that predate the inn?

Figure 37: The Williamsburg Inn: Do the Ghosts enjoy the "good life"?

Although I have never stayed at the inn, I have enjoyed the exquisite dining and would highly recommend it. I have only ever heard of paranormal activity in one room at the inn, which I understand is not rented out to guests. The inn has had a who's who list of guests, ranging from Queen Elizabeth, Ronald Reagan, Winston Churchill, Dwight Eisenhower, the Bushes, Emperor Hirohito of Japan, and Margaret Thatcher, to actors and TV personalities like Tom Selleck, Bill Cosby, John Travolta, Al Roker, Willard Scott, Matt Lauer, Colin Farrell, Alex Haley, Paula Deen, Robin Williams, Quincy Jones, Barbra Streisand, Betty White, and Joan Rivers. Wouldn't it be great if one or more of these apparitions were famous? I guess we'll never know . . .

One of the ironies of the grounds of Williamsburg's five-star accommodations for the wealthy is that somewhere nearby is the lost and unmarked graveyard of the paupers of the nineteenth and early twentieth centuries—lost to the annals of time. Evidence of these forgotten people may have showed up on my camera—both inside and outside this playground for the rich. Besides the group of five apparitions that dominate the sky over the Williamsburg Inn, I have captured many (and I mean *many*!) very obscure apparitions—mostly classic whites, both inside and outside the buildings that make up the inn. Could these be the castaway residents of Williamsburg's pauper cemetery? Obscure in life, is it coincidence that they are indistinct and difficult to see post-mortem? Unknown in life, how do they feel sharing their space with the rich and famous after their demise?

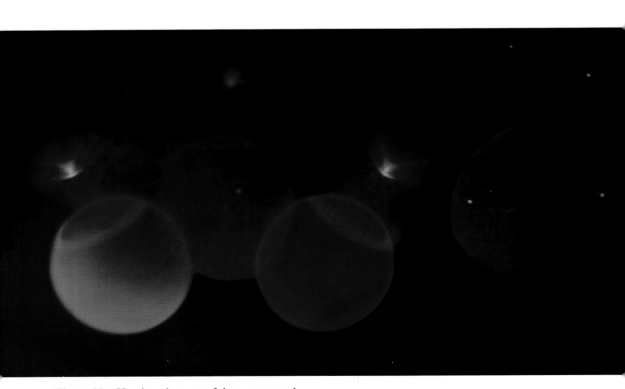

Figure 37a: Here's a close-up of the paranormal guests that hover over the Williamsburg Inn; I don't know if any of these guests were famous . . .

Figure 37b: A gathering of ghosts in one of the Williamsburg Inn's windows; are they from the lost pauper's graveyard nearby? Obscure in life, they are obscure in death—you have to look hard to see them. How many faces do you see?

This is one of the faces I found near the ground of the Williamsburg Inn; it was as if he was at the beach, buried up to his chest in sand.

This was the second face I found on the outside of the Inn; another ghost trying to make an appearance blocked his shoulders from sight.

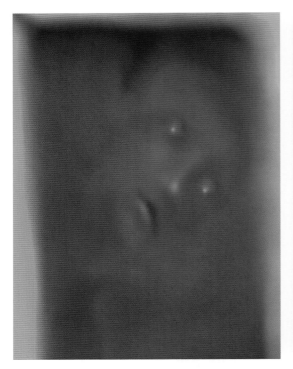

This is one of strangest and coolest of the Williamsburg Inn ghosts; no—the Blue Man Group is not missing a member . . .

The multi-colored hair was a surprise for this apparition, found in the same outside corner of the Williamsburg Inn as the others.

This is the Inn's Ghost Picasso; when I saw these two faces I thought—is it love, or is it a lover's quarrel? Perhaps Picasso got some of his ideas from seeing ghosts . . .

CHAPTER THIRTY-EIGHT

Alexander Craig House

Salacious Susanna the Spinster

History

With approximately 300 years of history, most of the houses in Colonial Williamsburg have had a number of owners. Since reciting all of the owners of each home that I have photographed would be absolutely mundane, I have only chosen the most noteworthy, appealing, and especially titillating characters in possession of the houses from its storied past. In the case of the original Alexander Craig House, two characters come to mind as worth mentioning: Alexander Craig and Susanna Allen—and they are about as different as night and day!

The original owner, a goldsmith, sold the property to Susanna Allen in 1712. Susanna first surfaced in Williamsburg in 1710, when she acquired a license to operate an ordinary at her house—wherever that was. But in her third year as an operator of an ordinary (bed and breakfast), she acquired this property and managed her business from here until her death in 1720. One year after Ms. Allen purchased this property, she was obligated to make a court appearance for some pretty serious charges: the first accusation she had to answer to was keeping the company of a married man, a serious charge in eighteenth-century colonial Virginia. The second charge needs a little background. A "disorderly house" would be known as a brothel or house of prostitution today. Evidently, Ms. Allen's ordinary was not very ordinary, pun intended. Imagine that, the capital of Virginia, full of politicians and businessmen, had a brothel! Well the grand jury convened and evidently did not find sufficient evidence for the charge of operating a "disorderly house." (Who knows, maybe some members of the grand jury were former customers!) But Ms. Allen did not dodge the bullet for the charge of keeping the company of a married man. The court found her guilty of that charge and deemed a heavy fine for her guilt: 500 pounds of tobacco. (Keep in mind that tobacco was used as currency in eighteenth-century Virginia—quite a fine for adultery!) Allen was found guilty, but no mention was made of who the married man was—double standard? I wonder if he helped pay the fine . . . Morality fines were paid to the wardens of the Bruton Parish Church, but evidently the guilty verdict was not grounds to keep Allen from managing an ordinary: the court provided her with an ordinary license the very next year. After her affair with the mysterious "married man," Susanna must not have found love—she died a spinster, a derisive eighteenth-century word for a woman who never married, a few years later in 1720. It's funny but the connotation of a spinster is a woman that never married and, therefore, never had sex, but the accusations in court were that Susanna led a salacious existence: a contradiction. By the way, keep Ms. Allen and her disorderly house in mind— we will come back to this in my next book.

The other owner of this house of interest, perhaps not as titillating as Ms. Susanna Allen, is the one for whom the house was named: Alexander Craig. Craig was a well-respected craftsman, who worked with leather, and according to the *Virginia Gazette*, "carried on the saddling business, in all its branches, to a greater extent than any one ever did before in this colony." Although he started his saddling business much earlier, Craig ran his business from this property from 1755 until his death in 1776. Eulogies appeared in all three Williamsburg papers for Craig, extolling his honesty, worth, and benevolence; indicative of his status in the community.

Craig's reputation in Williamsburg was quite stellar, in stark contrast to Ms. Susanna Allen, whose reputation was sullied by accusations of adultery and her business connected to prostitution. How much of her reputation she earned and how much was generated by rumor and possibly jealousy we will never know.

So, in this tale of two occupants, seemingly polar opposites, two different sides of the moral coin, who cannot bring themselves to leave? Are the members of the Craig family holding on to the past, or must Susanna Allen and some of her working girls relive a past they want to forget?

Salacious Spirits?

When I first photographed the Craig House, I was surprised to see so much activity overhead, as well as a lot of activity in the windows. I found one dominant spherical apparition, and from three to four Red Super Cells over the rather long house. There were several streaks of light (like in the window of the Wren Building) in three of the downstairs windows, as well as the faces that you will see on the next few pages. How much disorder these apparitions bring to this once-labeled disorderly house I do not know; whoever lives with these entities is just not talking. But I can't help but speculate that the woman whose face you see is Susanna Allen herself—the aforementioned spinster and accused adulteress. Is she looking for the love she never found, or perhaps the married man she was accused of keeping company with? Could one of the other ghosts be her companion in adultery, the man who was deemed innocent in life—is he judged culpable in death? Was Susanna's status sullied by the words of a jealous wife, or did she really earn her reputation as an adulteress and the madame of a brothel? Perhaps if you are brave enough, you can ask her—she prefers to appear in the downstairs far left window . . .

Figure 38: The Alexander Craig House, an original very early eighteenth-century house with a strange, triangular-shaped apparition overhead among quite a few others.

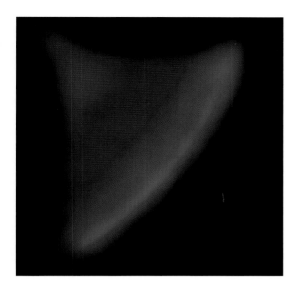

Figure 38a: The close-up, possibly a fountain-shaped apparition that's not fully formed?

Figure 38b: Is this strange female face with one normal eye and the other quite eerie the ghost of salacious Susanna, the owner of the not-so-ordinary "ordinary" that was Williamsburg's alleged brothel? Is she still looking for the married man she kept company with?

Figure 38c: This gentleman probably lived in this house in the nineteenth century; beards were not fashionable in the eighteenth century.

Figure 38d: I really don't know what to call this, but it's definitely paranormal and it definitely has what appears to be an angry look in its eyes. This is another example of something that looks more like an alien than a ghost. (Remember the side window in the Slaves' Quarters?) I think George Lucas would like to have this in his pantheon of *Star Wars* characters . . .

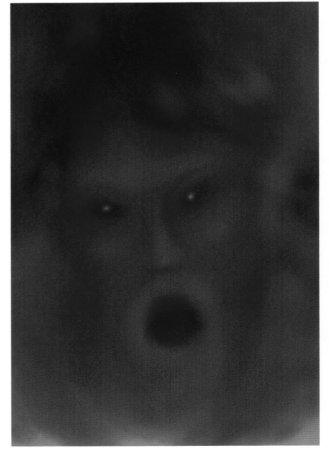

Figure 38e: Another gap-mouthed apparition whose facial hair indicates he was probably from the nineteenth century.

CHAPTER THIRTY-NINE

William Randolph House

The Shape-Shifting Apparition

Up until now, I had come to believe through the photographic evidence I have collected, that the Spherical Torch was a different type of entity from the Red Super Cell apparition. I don't think that "species" is an appropriate word here, but perhaps an analogy could be made between creatures made up of matter and those made up of energy; you would have different species for plants and animals, but what word could be used to classify the differences between these spirit creatures? Whatever word that is used for different types of apparitions, I've found photographic proof at the William Randolph house that these two seemingly different types of apparitions are really not: in a matter of seconds, from one photograph to the next, what was initially a Spherical Torch turned into a Red Super Cell apparition. Likewise, the apparition that is attached to the Spherical Torch, the Red Balloon, shape-shifted into the apparition that accompanies the Red Super Cell—a Yellow Unbrella. I would have to assume from these photographs, taken just seconds apart, that every Red Super Cell apparition can morph into a Spherical Torch and vice versa. Although it cannot change shape, a chameleon changes color for protection from predators. Perhaps the apparition changes both color and shape for movement; notice that in the first photo the Spherical Torch is by the second gable of the house, and in the second photo it is moving up and away to the left. In another photo taken several months later (after the house had been painted that reddish-brown color—the same color as the Peyton Randolph House—to indicate that the owner has wealth) the apparition has changed to a more elaborately shaped and brightly colored geo-light formation.

I also discovered a second anomaly at the William Randolph house: it is a reconstructed building, and yet it has a dominant apparition over the building. I have photographed apparitions over the area of the Governor's Palace as well as the Chiswell-Bucktrout house—but not over the buildings themselves—the apparitions were on the grounds of these two houses. However, the apparition at the William Randolph house was over the roof of the home—as if it was an original eighteenth-century house. Could it be that someone has died in the home since it was reconstructed, and that they are haunting the reconstructed home? Or is it possible that some part of the original house, or perhaps the foundation is what the spirit has attached itself to? Since I cannot answer either question, let's look at who William Randolph was and how he fit into the Williamsburg socio-political scene.

History

If you recall, the Peyton Randolph house is known as the most haunted house in Colonial Williamsburg—and not in a good way. This is the home of Peyton's Uncle William (Jr.), and is just a short walk down the street from Peyton's house. This house was originally built in 1737 for the use of William Randolph Jr. when he was at the capital serving in government; first as a member of the House of Burgesses for

Hanover County, as a member of the Governor's Council, as the treasurer for the Virginia Colony, and as Royal Councillor of State. His father, Col. William Randolph Sr. was one of the founders and original trustees for the College of William and Mary. William Randolph left three orphaned children when he died in 1742, and Thomas Jefferson's father, Peter, assumed responsibility for raising and caring for the Randolph children. Colonial Williamsburg rebuilt the house in 1949 to match as closely as possible the original home owned by William. So are the apparitions you will see on the next few pages from the Randolph family, or are they residents that lived in the rebuilt home after 1949? Since I am unfamiliar with the rules for haunting a particular house, I will leave you decide that conundrum.

I have not heard any ghost stories about this house, but as you can plainly see, there is

Figures 39 and 39a: The photographic evidence at the William Randolph House indicates that the Spherical Torch apparition can shape-shift into the Red Super Cell apparition in a matter of seconds. Is it for movement? In the first photograph the apparition is by the second gable, and in the second photo it is moving up and away from the house.

at least one dominant presence and a few characters in the windows (that you probably cannot see). Although I don't have a specific tale of a haunting, I have gone by this house at least fifty times in the past few years with the same result: I would find a Spherical Torch overhead and nothing in the windows—no faces, no classic whites, and nothing unusual. I did capture the dominant apparition, a Spherical Torch, which turned into a Red Super Cell as it moved away from the house. The change took only a few seconds, and my suspicions about these apparitions' shape-shifting abilities were finally recorded on camera. About six months later, I went on a hot August night, and it seemed like a plethora of faces showed up in the windows. Overhead, the dominant apparition was a very large, multi-colored geo-light apparition. It was as if they ignored me for three years, and finally just decided to show up.

Figure 39b: About six months later I took a photo of the William Randolph House that amazed me with the dazzling geo-light apparition—a first at this house. When I looked in the right front window, quite an array of characters showed up, with the clearest of them on the next few Figures.

Figure 39c: This couple was the first of the apparitions that caught my eye at the William Randolph House.

Figure 39d: The second face that I noted was this old man with the wild, unruly hair and the piercing eyes. The beard suggests Civil War era . . .

Figure 39e: This may be another character from the Civil War years; perhaps he has even got on a uniform . . . it appears that there is another bearded man trying to make an appearance behind this man's head.

CHAPTER FORTY

Benjamin Powell House

The Undertaker

History

Benjamin Powell was a carpenter who later became a building contractor, which back in the eighteenth century was called an "undertaker." He purchased this property in 1763, and his next "undertaking" was to build this home. Some of his most notable jobs as a contractor were the repairing of the jail (gaol) in 1764, building the Williamsburg Hospital (asylum) in 1771, and the construction of an original structure that you can still see today: the steeple tower at the Bruton Parish Church in 1769. Powell served on a committee in 1774 that enforced the embargo on British goods, along with other Williamsburg notables, such as George Wythe and Peyton Randolph.

Insights

The Powell house is on the edge of the tiny capital, and doesn't see much traffic. It's not very well lit at night, and as a result, it doesn't appear to have too much paranormal activity. What I've discovered as I've said is that "ghosts," (or however you would like to refer to them) like artificial light, people, and noise. The Powell House does not get much of that, and as a result, you only see one orb over the building. I did

find several faces in the upstairs windows, but even these were not very bright. I have consistently found that ghosts usually do not manifest themselves unless there is activity in or around the home. The George Wythe House is a perfect example: the only time I can find any apparitions in or around that house is when there are special evening programs being held inside the house, and sometimes (just sometimes) when there is a large ghost tour outside the house. Otherwise the place sits in stony silence, as if nothing out of the ordinary ever goes on in the place—and nothing shows up on the photographs that I take. I believe the same thing goes for the Benjamin Powell House, as you will see on the next couple of pages. Most of the time, the parallel universe of the paranormal is in hibernation, but sometimes, with a little outside activity, I can find something there that is not of this material world. I've found new meaning in the phrase "make enough noise to wake the dead . . ." Take a look at the next few pages; I roused these entities from a period of slumber or inactivity. Out of these different visages, I wonder if any of them are Benjamin Powell himself—or are they just anonymous owners or boarders who have spent enough time in this house to call it their post-mortem home . . .

Figure 40: Here is the Benjamin Powell House, sitting quietly on the outskirts of the Colonial Capital, with just one medium-sized orb relaxing on the roof. I wonder if it is incapable of appearing as anything brighter (such as a Spherical Torch or Red Super Cell) because of the lack of sufficient ambient light? I also found other tenants in the upstairs gable windows that were as dimly lit as the house.

Figure 40a: Here is one of the present residents in the upstairs portion of the Benjamin Powell House; perhaps you would like to spend the evening with him? The house seems to be rather quiet and inactive, but who knows what would happen if you were a part of a group that spent the night upstairs—remember that he would be staying in the upstairs bedroom with you . . .

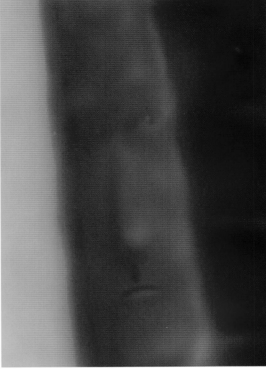

Figure 40b: This guy looks a little more innocuous; could this be the "undertaker" Benjamin Powell? (I'm not sure why, but the eyes are unusually small—if anything these apparitions usually have over-sized eyes!)

Figure 40c: This apparition appeared to the side of the upstairs window—shaped like the elongated space that it showed up in.

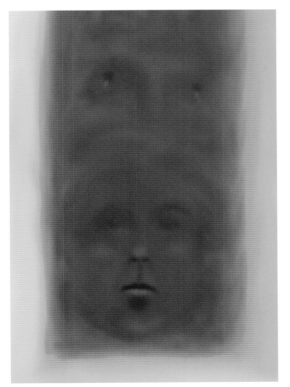

Figure 40d: Finally these two showed up in one windowpane to complete the cast of characters at the quietest house this side of Colonial Williamsburg.

CHAPTER FORTY-ONE

Masonic Hall

Where is Peyton?

Williamsburg's first official Masonic Lodge, or "hall" as it was originally called, was dedicated in 1778 and stood until 1910 at which time it was deemed irreparable. The building was replaced in 1931 with a new building that included the bricks from the old foundation incorporated into the first floor's fireplace. Although this is the first official permanent meeting place for the Masons in Williamsburg, they had existed in Williamsburg much earlier in the eighteenth century. In fact, the *Virginia Gazette* carried an article as early as 1737, probably written by a Mason in defense of the organization. This article, as well as one written in 1751 referring to the Masonic Lodge in the city "some time ago" indicates that the Masons were in Williamsburg at least by the 1730s. But since the official records do not exist to reflect this early existence, Williamsburg does not get credit for Virginia's first Masonic Hall—Norfolk does. Nevertheless, the popularity of Freemasonry by the founding fathers of the United States, including many that either lived in Williamsburg or came here as a participant in the political machinations of the Virginia colony, assured a strong membership up until and during the American Revolution. About 100 members of the Williamsburg chapter actually fought in the War for Independence.

But before the Masons had an official place to meet, they met at the taverns in Williamsburg. The Crown Tavern is the first place on official record as the meeting place for the brotherhood, with a familiar character in charge in 1762: Grand Master Peyton Randolph. Yes, the man who was an important Williamsburg attorney, attorney general for the Virginia colony, speaker of the Virginia House of Burgesses, president of the First Continental Congress, and the first man to be called the "father of our country," was also the leader of Masonic Lodge in Williamsburg. Isn't it intriguing that the former owner of Williamsburg's most haunted house, interred in the family crypt of the oldest, most haunted college building (still in use) in the country, is the former leader of Virginia's most haunted Masonic lodge? Would you like to take a guess who the primary suspect is in the haunting of Mason Hall #6? Without giving or taking away any credence to the belief throughout the members of the lodge that Peyton is the paranormal perpetrator—let me suggest another possibility— because there are more than one . . .

After the American Revolution, there were several periods when the Williamsburg Masonic Lodge went dark. The first devastating event to the membership of the lodge was the removal of the capital to Richmond; many people moved with the capital to its new site. The result was that the organization became inactive during the 1790s; after a brief reopening, the lights went out again sometime between 1802 and 1811. After another revival, the lodge went dark once more because of a scandal: circa 1827–1828, the William Morgan Affair erupted. William Morgan was a Mason who threatened to write an expose revealing secrets of the brotherhood. Morgan was kidnapped and murdered, and the public blamed Morgan's Masonic fraternity. The public outcry gave rise to an anti-Masonic sentiment that was so strong it developed into a short-lived political party, aptly named the Anti-Masonic Party. The party was only capable of supporting one presidential candidate before dying a quick death, but Williamsburg #6 did not reopen until 1848. The very first Grand Lodge of Virginia has been able to stay open since that date—however, sporadically during the Union occupation of Williamsburg from 1862—1865.[10]

I hadn't planned to include the Masonic Lodge in this book because it is not an original eighteenth-century building, but when a friend of mine just happened to mention a haunting, I listened. I asked him if they (the Masons) knew who the ghost was, and he immediately replied, "Yeah, it's Peyton Randolph." As soon as I heard that name, I was immediately intrigued. The man who owned the most haunted house in Williamsburg was haunting the Masonic Temple? He said that whenever anyone enters the building, they always acknowledge the ghost, saying, "Hi Peyton; it's just us!" He also mentioned that things are moved all of the time, and they have to go looking for these items on a regular basis. Peyton did have one of the usual prerequisites to becoming a ghost—a sudden, unexpected death. He was in Philadelphia at the time for the third Continental Congress when he had a massive stroke and died. He was

brought back to Williamsburg, greeted by his Masonic brothers, and he was interred in one of the crypts at the Wren Chapel with his father.

Perhaps he did return to the lodge, but I wonder if anyone thought of the possibility that William Morgan may have returned to his old haunt? Evidently there is room enough for more than just two: I found between four and five apparitions over temple #6, and a few faces in the windows. Peyton Randolph was a portly man, and I captured a portly man in a photo, but I can't definitively identify him as the former grand master. Neither can I say if one of the other faces is the aforementioned William Morgan or not, but nevertheless these visages are among the paranormal occupants of the temple. Perhaps not in life, but in death, Peyton Randolph is tied to the most haunted in Williamsburg: The most haunted residence, the most haunted university building, and the most paranormally active Masonic Hall. Care to join?

Endnotes

10. Brinkley, M. Kent. "History of Williamsburg Lodge #6, A.F. & A.M., Williamsburg Masonic Lodge," March 1, 1999, accessed January 15, 2015, http://williamsburgva6.com/history.html.

Figure 41: The Masonic Hall #6 in Williamsburg, with just one of the four to five apparitions visible at this angle.

Figure 41a: Shooting at a different angle, you will see three to four Red Super Cells hanging at the gable on the far left of the building, just like the Nicholson House.

Figure 41b: Below the apparition in figure 41a is another at the center right gable window. The verdict: the Masonic Temple has more than the usual share of ghosts, but which one is Peyton Randolph?

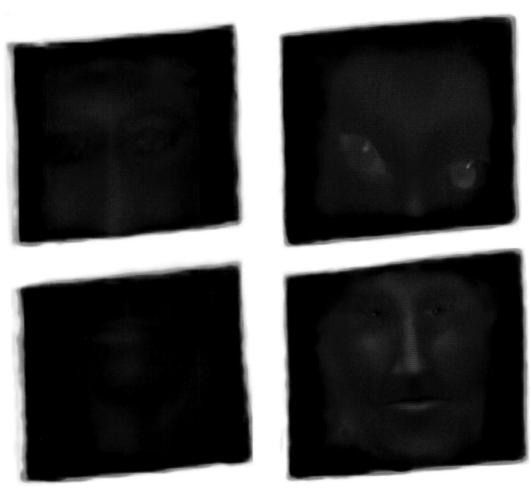

Figure 41c: The face that appeared in the upstairs gable window—a rather intimidating look, wouldn't you say? From what I've seen so far, it seems that when a face appears in more than one windowpane, it looks elongated—what do you think?

Figure 41d: In the bottom pane you can see the overweight man that may or may not be the apparition of Peyton Randolph. The top apparition is an unknown person that appears to be much younger with strange looking eyes.

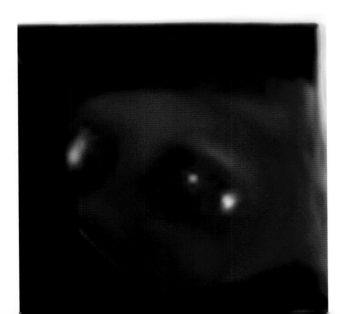

Figure 41e: To the left you can see something a bit more bizarre—a wide-eyed charcoal grey ghost.

CHAPTER FORTY-TWO

Hunter Millinery

Phantoms for Fashion

Fashion in the eighteenth century was just floor-length gowns and hats for women and tricorner hats, waistcoats, breeches, and wigs for men, right? The 1700s, contrary to what many think, was a time when fashion changed constantly, and the middle and upper classes came to the Margaret Hunter Millinery to stay current with the latest English fashion. (What better way to keep the money flowing into the coffers of milliners in Paris, London, and the colonies than to keep changing the fashion—most people think that idea developed in the twentieth century!)

Although one of the main functions of a millinery was to sell clothing accessories, the store's product lines went beyond clothing to include fashion accessories for the home, making the millinery a forerunner for the modern department store. The word "millinery" originally came from merchants trying to imitate the stores in Milan, Italy, which sold products such as silk from the Orient, clothing, ribbons, weapons, armor, and other fashionable goods. The period after the Great Fire of London in 1655 led to some changes in the merchandise at the millinery; shopkeepers began to offer many different products, and millinery referenced the French word for "thousand"—*mille*—indicative of the thousands of different products now for sale in these shops. Letters discovered by Colonial Williamsburg researchers indicate that the upper class Virginians were more

fashion conscious and dressed better than the people in London, who, in turn, were preoccupied with French fashion.

This store was built sometime between 1735 and 1755, and the Hunter sisters (Jane, and later her sister, Margaret) are listed as the ones creating the fashionable clothing at this store. If newspaper advertisements are a good indicator of the years the Hunter Millinery was in the fashion business, then we're looking at the period from 1767 to 1780. After Margaret Hunter died in 1787, details are sketchy at best, but the building continued as a storefront (downstairs) and lodging (upstairs) of some sort up until the Civil War. By 1861, the shop had been enlarged to two stories, and continued to be a store until the early twentieth century, when it was converted to an auto shop. Colonial Williamsburg removed the second story and all of the other changes made through the years to return it to its eighteenth-century appearance. The only original features are the foundation and the east and west walls, evidently enough for the shop's paranormal residents.

Two of the apparitions captured look more like they were connected to the auto shop than the fashion business; a third looks like a youth who has lost all of his hair—a fatal illness? The first photo of the shop shows another gigantic apparition (to the far right) like the ones at the Wren Building, leaving me to wonder: Did something that big come out of one person?

Figure 42. This photograph shows three apparitions, one that is super-sized and similar to the gigantic apparition seen at the Wren Building on the campus of William and Mary.

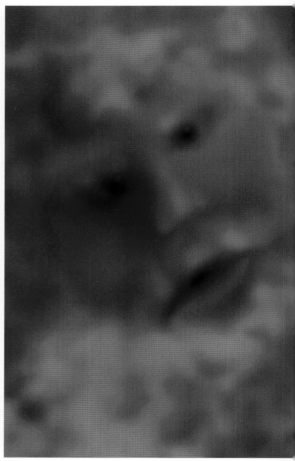

Figure 42a: Insurance policies on this building indicate that it continued to be a store throughout the nineteenth century, changing hands seven times until 1843. The store continued and was enlarged, eventually becoming an auto repair shop. These next two apparitions may have been part of this revolving door of owners; I found two bearded apparitions next to each other in the second floor window of this store.

Figure 42b: The second bearded apparition appeared in the same pane as the first, right next to it, as if they were friends or brothers in life. This fellow looks like an angry Santa.

Figure 42c: This apparition was in another windowpane, along with all of its smaller companion faces. How many faces do you see besides the large one?

CHAPTER FORTY-THREE

Churches—a Hotbed for Paranormal Activity?

A Gathering of the Faithful . . . or the Unfaithful?

History

After finding so much paranormal activity at the Bruton Parish Church, I wondered if I would have the same success with other historical churches. So I tried the Hickory Neck Episcopal Church, a church that is just a little younger than Bruton: Hickory Neck was built in 1734, with a northern transept built in 1774. It was the site of an encampment of American Revolutionary War soldiers in April of 1781 and, in August, was put into use as an army hospital—effectively ending the building's use as a church for many years. This was a state-owned church, and after the Revolutionary War ended, the newly formed government disestablished a government-sanctioned religion. The state still owned the church and the property and decided to put it to public use—as a school. But for some reason the state demolished the main body of the church (the portion built in 1734) and left the addition (built in 1774) to be used as a public school, doubling on the weekend as a church by various denominations. The school, known as the Hickory Neck Academy, was in disrepair after the Civil War ended, and beginning in 1871, repairs began to be made. The building was used as a school until 1908, when a new high school was constructed in Toano. In 1912, the church and the property was given back to the Episcopal Church, and the rector of Bruton Parish Church, E. Ruffin Jones, worked towards the restoration and use of the eighteenth-century building as an Episcopal Church again. He succeeded, and

the little church resumed its original role in 1915 as a church, with Episcopal worship services resuming for the first time in many years. The building was consecrated again as a place of worship in 1917 and placed on the National Registry for Historic Places in 1973. A new church was built in 2006, ending for the second time the use of this historic building as a place of worship, but as you will see in the photographs on the next few pages, there are a few holdouts, unwilling to leave the old church and school. Perhaps that has to do with the gravesites outside . . .[11]

Narrative

Although it may look that way in the photograph, the moon was not quite full the night I chose to photograph the old Episcopal Church. It was very helpful in giving me a little light, because the sides and back of the church were very dark, and it was very difficult to see without it. As you can probably tell, the front has spotlights on it, but that doesn't help much on the other three sides. I immediately saw the Yellow Umbrella and the Red Super Cell upon reviewing the photo, but I could not see the small sphere on top of the roof. I also would have to magnify the photo to find some of the characters that still reside in and around this historic building. Although I never sensed anything, the next photograph that I took was right where you see the Red Super Cell apparition; perhaps it moved, or perhaps I walked right through it . . .

Hickory Neck has a gallery of faces that may intrigue you; it also has several things not seen before. I discovered two women dressed in long gowns, one facing and one with her back to the camera—and both were missing their left arm. On top of the church sits a strange apparition that looks like a large, blood-shot eye with a large, blue pupil. There is a cast of characters that include men with long beards, probably circa-Civil War, and one of the most profoundly sad faces I think I have ever captured. An apparition that looks like a windsock rounds

out the Hickory Neck gallery; from there we move on to the Mathew's Baptist Church, formed in 1776, with some of the largest apparitions seen since the College of William and Mary's Wren Building. As if that's not enough to prove that churches are a hotbed for the paranormal, we return to Bruton for more proof . . .

Endnotes

11. History of Hickory Neck, Hickory Neck Episcopal Church, Accessed December 5, 2015, www. hickoryneck.org/hne-faq.

Figure 43: The historic Hickory Neck Episcopal Church on a night when the moon could help illuminate my movement around the very dark sides and back of the building. Notice the Yellow Umbrella to the left, the Red Super Cell to the right, the small sphere at the top of the roof, and the magical lights in the small shrub at the bottom right. (Did you ever wonder where the idea for fairies came from?)

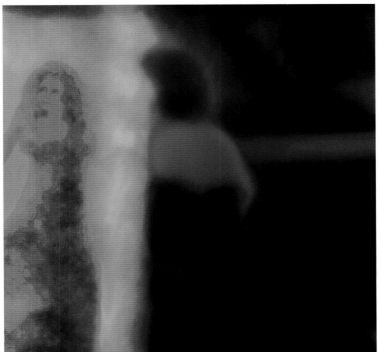

Figure 43a: In the lower left window, I came across two women that appear to be facing each other. They are both in long dresses, perhaps for church, a wedding, or a funeral? Both apparitions do not have a left arm. Behind the brunette you may be able to see what appears to be the head of an older man looking down at both women from about a 45-degree angle—can you see him?

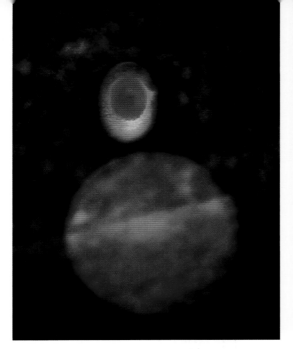

Figure 43b: This orb sat on top of the church, but needed a boost in contrast to be seen clearly. It is much smaller than the dominant spherical orbs you may be used to seeing throughout the latter half of this book, and rather than a "torch"-type light at the top of the apparition, there is something that resembles a bloodshot blue eye.

Figure 43c: I found a trio of faces looking at me from one of the windowpanes at Hickory Neck Church; the beard on the man on the left suggests a ghost from the nineteenth century—possibly from the Civil War battle for Williamsburg (Fort Magruder).

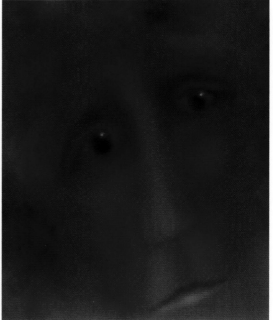

Figure 43d: Here's the third face I captured in the windowpane just above the two faces from Figure 43c at Hickory Neck Church; like the other gentleman, this heavily bearded man is likely from the Civil War era. I wonder if they are all related . . . or just random faces thrown together by war.

Figure 43e: This ghost looks incredibly despondent; it makes you wonder just what kind of mortal experience could weigh so heavily on him post-mortem?

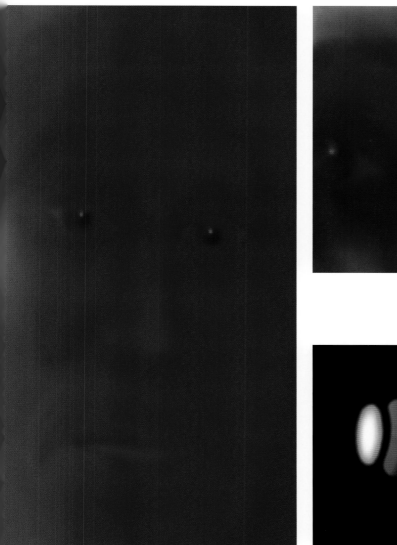

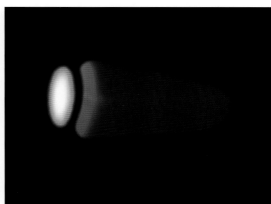

Figure 43f: Another forlorn phantom looks out at the living from the confines of the Hickory Neck Church.

Figure 43g: A newly discovered apparitional shape—it looks like a windsock!

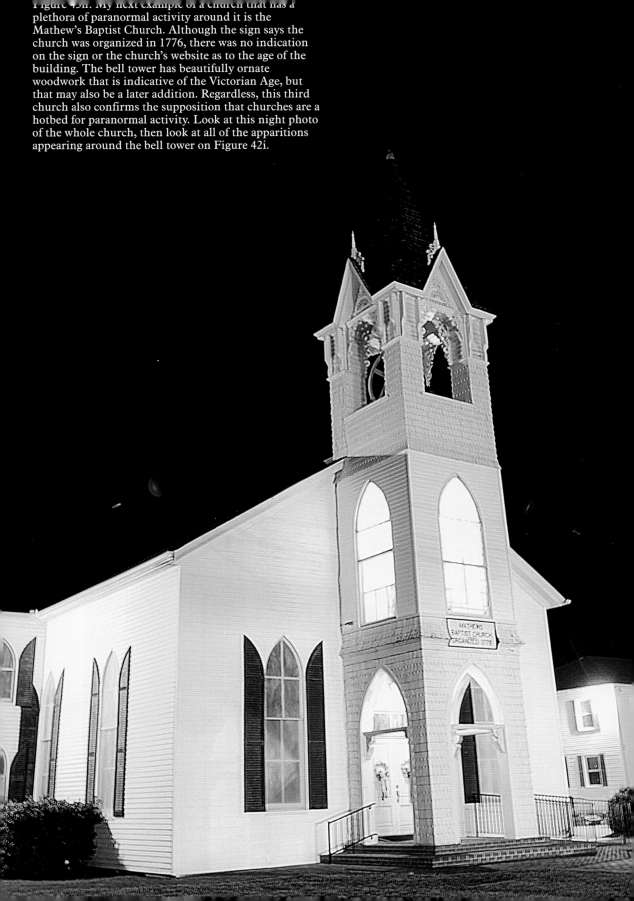

Figure 43h. My next example of a church that has a plethora of paranormal activity around it is the Mathew's Baptist Church. Although the sign says the church was organized in 1776, there was no indication on the sign or the church's website as to the age of the building. The bell tower has beautifully ornate woodwork that is indicative of the Victorian Age, but that may also be a later addition. Regardless, this third church also confirms the supposition that churches are a hotbed for paranormal activity. Look at this night photo of the whole church, then look at all of the apparitions appearing around the bell tower on Figure 42i.

Figure 43i: The view of just the bell tower of the Mathew's Baptist Church and all of the paranormal activity going on around it. On each side of the bell tower, you can see only a quarter of two gigantic red apparitions that are larger than the whole bell tower—what on earth could that be? I took this photograph sometime between 1:00 and 2:00 a.m. on a Sunday morning; I don't know if they all gathered for a party on Saturday night or are just early for Sunday morning services. I thought Bruton Parish Church had a lot of apparitions, but the number and size of these apparitions just amazed me; I still can't help but wonder what the two gigantic apparitions are and were.

Bruton Parish Church Revisited

Bruton Parish Church is where my journey began, and it's where I first found an apparition that I thought was just beautiful. I wondered if this apparition, the "Spirit Fountain," had made the changeover to a circular shape like all of the other apparitions I had photographed before April 27, so I went back to where I started—and I was shocked to see the changes that occurred!

I thought it would be fitting to end my journey where I started, and as you will find out, it's a great place to end. The guardian of the church has become spherical, but much brighter and more intricate than the other apparitions that have undergone a metamorphosis into the round. The warm weather seems to have brought out more apparitions to float around the steeple tower.

Figure 43j: The guardian of the Bruton Parish Church, undergoing a complete metamorphosis from its shape at the beginning of the book to a spherical shape. It appears as if it's a standoff between the guardian and the Red Super Cell orb.

Figure 43k: As is the case with all of the photos, I cannot turn up the contrast on the whole picture to bring out the apparitions without washing out the whole photograph. But after I crop this photo and turn up the contrast, you can see what a magnificent apparition guards the Bruton Parish Church— probably the most elaborate form in the whole book, and I think there was more below the roof!

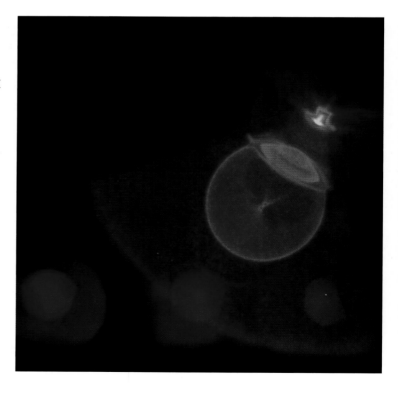

Figure 431: When the guardian is not hovering directly over the church, it seems that the other orbs like to come out and play. The Yellow Umbrellas look like they are floating merrily around the bell tower, as the Red Super Cell orbs look on from a higher vantage point, and the grays just floating by without a care.

What I've Learned About "Ghosts"

Trying to Understand the Unseen, the Unheard & the Unknown

After taking thousands of photos (the great thing about digital cameras is that you can delete, and I have used that feature frequently) trying to capture these anomalies of light, I've learned a few things about them.

The first thing that I learned came from my first capture: it seems that the apparitions are only visible from one direction. If you recall, I captured my first photo at the Bruton Parish Church, but I could only capture the apparition on the one side of the church—facing due north. When I faced northwest or even west, I could not capture anything but the building. Perhaps the apparitions are only two dimensional instead of three; or if they encompass more than two dimensions, they are not ones that we can see or are even aware of. The same thing happened at the St. George Tucker House. I tried quite a few times from the back of the house, because there are no trees there, giving an unobstructed view of the whole house—but to no avail. This apparition can only be captured from the front of the house (again facing due north). Ditto for the Travis House. That doesn't mean that it has to be due north; the anomaly at the Whetherburn Tavern was facing due south and the one at the Roscow Cole House was facing due west. (Williamsburg was laid out like a grid, with streets going east to west (like the city's main street, the Duke of Gloucester Street), or north to south (like the two streets leading to the Governor's Palace, on either side of the Palace Green).

Something else that I've noticed is that these entities seem to go into a state of inactivity (hibernation, suspended animation, whatever you would like to call it). They seem to be attracted to (artificial or moon) light and noise, the way humans are—perhaps that wakes them up. The Roscow Cole House is a good example: Around Christmas, Colonial Williamsburg will have evening programs that include its Fife and Drum Corps and choirs singing traditional (eighteenth century and before, in keeping with the colonial time period) Christmas songs or hymns. Such a program was going on at the Courthouse of 1770 when I captured the apparition on the rooftop of the Roscow Cole House, which faces the courthouse where the program was unfolding. The Fife and Drum Corps marched up the Duke of Gloucester Street to the front of the courthouse and played several tunes, then the choir sang the Christmas hymns. During the program, the apparition stayed on the rooftop, giving me the impression that it too was observing the Christmas event. When the program ended, the apparition began to ascend up into the sky till I could no longer see it. I don't know how far up into the sky or heavens these creatures go, but I have a series of photographs showing this apparition moving upward. Counter that with the Whetherburn Tavern, where I saw the creature (through a series of photographs) descend to see the activity on the street.

I prefer not to speculate on what these creatures are, though I've been pressed to do so. Whether they are departed human spirits, angels, or demons, I do not know. I am a Christian, and have had Christian fundamentalists come to me urging caution—saying that these creatures could only be demons and that I must be careful. I have accompanied others who claim to have psychic abilities; they say that these are the souls of humans who are lingering here because they have been wronged, murdered, or are otherwise a lost soul because of some tragic event in their life. I prefer to remain objective and open to all points of view, although I would hope that not all of these creatures are evil or demonic. The Peyton Randolph House seems to be the only place where there is something truly malicious; in all of the other places the creatures seem to be innocuous—even the jail. If they were all demonic, would they not all be malevolent? Would they not have some sort of evil agenda? What could they possibly gain by pretending to be the lost soul of a human? Just trying to reason my thoughts out on paper; although the explanation that makes most sense to me would be the souls of humans that continue to live on after death, I just don't know. So I choose to remain open-minded about the answer, and I still exercise caution when I'm out. Whether these apparitions are a part of us (as a soul) or a completely different creature, they are both interesting and frightening at the same time; because as you know, we are afraid of what we do not understand, especially if it is more intelligent and powerful than we are.

One thing I do know: They move—lightning fast when they want to, they react to their environment, and they alter their appearance—a shape-shifter in the true sense of the word. They have periods of rest, or at least inactivity. Most of the apparitions appear on the roof or hover over the roof—almost always near the chimney—of the home they are, for the lack of a better word, haunting. The exceptions are the Peyton Randolph House, the George Wythe House, and the Williamsburg Gaol (Jail). They vary in appearance from a very simple, small grey circle, or orb, to a very large, multi-colored, beautifully shaped light anomaly. They seem to be capable of appearing as their former human selves (if they are lost human souls) or as former occupants of the houses they appear in (if they are either angels or demons). I have only used recognizable faces in the windows of the houses

and buildings in Colonial Williamsburg, but trust me, there are a lot more—often distorted and unrecognizable. I have been able to verify some of the legacies and ghost stories in Colonial Williamsburg, but some I have completely missed: for example, the elusive "snow angel" apparition that appears at the Geddy House has appeared as a woman in Civil War era attire in windows for both tourists and Colonial Williamsburg employees alike. A very pale woman dressed in black appears every now and then for the tourists during the evenings out in front of the St. George Tucker House.

Whenever they show their faces in the windows, other smaller faces that are likewise trying to appear and be recognized often accompany them; sometimes all they can manifest is a multitude of eyes. It's almost like these houses have multiple spirits in them that are in competition with each other to be recognized. I wonder if the ability to project a face is something that they have to learn how to do—and consequently some are better than others at creating a likeness of their former selves. However, rather than competing to be seen, sometimes spirits will pool their energy together to create an apparition that is much bigger than what they could make individually. The best example of that is the large apparition that resembled the figure of a man in the tree to the right of the President's House.

I had one possible encounter with one of these apparitions at the Bruton Parish Church. The first photo that I took, the apparition was hovering about ten or more feet above the roof. In the next few photographs that I took, the apparition was descending—towards me! After it descended below the rooftop, I could no longer make out the characteristic shape that I had seen before (see Chapter 1)—I believed the artificial lights washed it out. But I did see a bluish tint in the light from the streetlamp that I had not seen before. I operate my camera with a remote control after I have set the controls and focused the lens. When I took the final picture, I had my flash on. The second the flash went off, it looked like someone threw glitter up into the air all around me, and I felt a chill down my back. I came to the conclusion that the creature was right there in front of me—and possibly checking me out; but after witnessing the glittery reflection from the flash of my camera, I could see nothing else with the naked eye. Unfortunately, the camera was not able to pick anything up either, so I had no real evidence or proof that the entity was right there in front of me, just a visceral feeling. I have seen the glitter other times when I have used the flash, but I did not have evidence of an apparition approaching me like the time at the Bruton Parish Church; but then again, one could be following me. I really don't know exactly what I'm dealing with, but it's equal parts intriguing and frightening at the same time.

I have come to another conclusion: Apparitions seem to prefer to hang out near chimneys. Is it the heat—are they drawn to the heat? Someone suggested that the chimney is an easy way into the home, which is true. If they are creatures made up of pure energy (as opposed to matter), I thought that would enable them to travel through solid objects—in this case walls or roofs—but perhaps that would take more energy to do so. Don't ask me what happens at homes or buildings without chimneys; I don't know . . . yet. It's kind of like Santa Claus at Christmas—only this is all year-round for these creatures.

I have noticed that when I felt like there was a "presence" near me, I believe it gives me chills because it is absorbing the heat from my body. So I do not feel that they are *cold creatures,* they just seem cold because they are sucking the heat energy right out of our bodies, just like some ghosts have learned to suck the energy right out of batteries. I can only wonder if that is their food—or how they sustain life—by absorbing energy. All creatures need some kind of energy to sustain life; I wonder if that is their lifeline as they hover over and around these houses and other buildings like sentinels, guarding and looking over what was once theirs—and maybe still is . . .

Along the same lines I wondered why these creatures seem to be more active at night or in the early morning hours. If they need to absorb energy to sustain life, then perhaps they use the daylight hours as a period of rest and renewal—

by absorbing life-giving energy from the sun. As I mentioned before, they are still attracted to artificial light and seem to prefer to hang out near man-made light sources. The fact that I witnessed an apparition projecting his appearance onto an electronic device makes me believe that they know more than we think they do: they may have died hundreds of years ago, but they are savvy enough to know that electronic devices have batteries to drain and they also have the technical know-how to transmit their image onto a complex network of circuitry and make their likeness appear on a laptop or cell phone.

I also believe that the Red Balloon, the lower part of the spherical apparition that is always on the house, is the sensory center of this creature. I believe that it is like the eyes and ears of the apparition so that it can keep close tabs on what's going on inside the house as it stands guard over the outside. The Yellow Umbrellas serve the same purpose for the Red Super Cell apparitions. I do know that the Red Balloon is only ever one to two meters away from the Spherical Torch apparitions, the Yellow Umbrellas are likewise connected to the Red Super Cells, but they can be seen much farther away—five to ten meters or more.

Something else that I wonder about is that when they do notice me aiming my camera at the house or building they occupy or "haunt," do they light up because they want to be seen or recognized, or is it a defensive measure? In other words, do they intensify their light as warning, as if to say, "Stay away; this is my place"? Or are they trying to say, "Look at me; I'm here. I've been here for several hundred years, and I would like to be recognized."

"The Light"

I know that you've heard stories about people who have literally stopped breathing and were pronounced clinically dead; they say that they felt themselves leave their bodies and go towards "the light." Inevitably, in order for them to tell this story, they have had to not go into the light but return to their bodies. After seeing these photographs of these beautiful light apparitions,

I wonder if the real story is not "going into the light," *but becoming the light.*

Likewise I have heard all of the Biblical references about the light—always thinking that it was purely metaphorical. Perhaps it's more than a metaphor, but an actual reference to a being made up of light. (I'm not saying there is not a metaphorical reference, but I'm saying that the reference is made because these creatures are made up of energy that gives off light.) Maybe these references are made as metaphorical, but *based* on the physical makeup of these spirit creatures. For example, the psalmist wrote that God "wraps himself in light as with a garment" (Psalm 104: 2). In another place Jesus says, "I am the light of the world"; another reference to both metaphorical light and real light? I have heard references to God as well as the comments made by people who have clinically died; after taking these photos, those words have a new meaning . . .

I hope you've had as much fun discovering the paranormal as I have! Whatever your religious beliefs or views of an afterlife, these photos point to the existence of something that we can't fully explain or understand. The variety of shapes and colors reminds me of the variety of life on earth; and like fingerprints and snowflakes—no two are exactly alike. So remember the next time you go hunting for ghosts, or perhaps go on a "ghost tour," the ghosts you are looking for are probably right overhead—watching you . . .

Bibliography

Primary Sources

Olmart, Michael, Suzanne E. Coffman, and Paul, Aron. *Official Guide to Colonial Williamsburg.* Third Edition. Williamsburg, VA: The Colonial Williamsburg Foundation, 2007. www.history.org.

Additional Sources

Behrend, Jackie Eileen. *The Haunting of Williamsburg, Yorktown, and Jamestown.* Winston-Salem, NC: John F. Blair Publisher, 1999.

Brinkley, M. Kent. History of Williamsburg Lodge #6, A.F. & A.M., Williamsburg Masonic Lodge. (March 1, 1999 / Accessed January 15, 2015) http://williamsburgva6.com/history.html.

Dickens, Charles. *A Christmas Carol.* London, England: Chapman & Hall, 1843.

History of Hickory Neck, Hickory Neck Episcopal Church. (Accessed December 5, 2015) www.hickoryneck.org/hne-faq/.

Hume, Ivor Noel. Doctor Goodwin's Ghosts, Colonial Williamsburg Foundation. (Accessed November 17, 2014) www.history.org/foundation/journal/spring01/wythe_ghosts.cfm?showSite=mobile

Rouse, Parke, Henry Hair Buyer Hamilton. *Daily Press* (February 16, 1992/Accessed September 27, 2015) http://articles.dailypress.com/1992-02-16/news/9202170126_1_british-ohio-valley-sir-henry-hamilton.

Sheehan, Bernard W. "The Famous Hair Buyer General: Henry Hamilton, George Rogers Clark, and the American Indian." (Accessed September 27, 2015) scholarworks.dlib.indiana.edu.

Slawinski, Jansz. "Electromagnetic Radiation and the Afterlife, New Dualism Archive." (1987 / Accessed March 25, 2015) PDF document available online: http://www.newdualism.org.

Taylor, L. B. Jr. *The Ghosts of Williamsburg . . . and Nearby Environs.* Williamsbrg, VA: L. B. Taylor Jr., 1983.